COCKTA...

COLLECTED SHEET MUSIC: COOL AND SWINGIN'

PIANO • VOCAL • GUITAR

MW01410398

Produced by
Alfred Music Publishing Co., Inc.
P.O. Box 10003
Van Nuys, CA 91410-0003
alfred.com

Printed in USA.

No part of this book shall be reproduced, arranged, adapted, recorded, publicly performed, stored in a retrieval system, or transmitted by any means without written permission from the publisher. In order to comply with copyright laws, please apply for such written permission and/or license by contacting the publisher at alfred.com/permissions.

ISBN-10: 0-7390-7962-X
ISBN-13: 978-0-7390-7962-1

Cover photo: Cocktail © iStockphoto.com / chihhang

 Alfred Cares. Contents printed on 100% recycled paper.

CONTENTS

TITLE	ARTIST	PAGE
As Time Goes By	Dooley Wilson	4
At Last	Etta James	8
Begin the Beguine	Artie Shaw and His Orchestra	13
The Best Is Yet to Come	Frank Sinatra	20
Blue Moon	The Mavericks	25
Blueberry Hill	Fats Domino	30
Come Rain or Come Shine	Frank Sinatra	38
Days of Wine and Roses	Andy Williams	42
Desperado	Eagles	44
Don't Get Around Much Anymore	Duke Ellington	50
Drinking Again	Frank Sinatra	35
Dream a Little Dream of Me	The Mamas & the Papas	54
Escape (The Piña Colada Song)	Rupert Holmes	57
Faithfully	Journey	62
Hit the Road Jack	Ray Charles	66
Home	Michael Bublé	74
How Deep Is Your Love	Bee Gees	71
How Do You Keep the Music Playing?	James Ingram and Patti Austin	80
Human Nature	Michael Jackson	85
I Get a Kick Out of You	Frank Sinatra	92
If You Don't Know Me by Now	Simply Red	100
It Had to Be You	Harry Connick, Jr.	97
I've Got a Crush on You	Linda Ronstadt	106
I've Got You Under My Skin	Frank Sinatra	110
Just One of Those Things	Ella Fitzgerald	122
Killing Me Softly with His Song	Roberta Flack	116
The Lady Is a Tramp	Frank Sinatra	127
Laura	Frank Sinatra	132
Let's Call the Whole Thing Off	Billie Holiday	142

TITLE	ARTIST	PAGE
Let's Do It (Let's Fall in Love)	Ella Fitzgerald	137
Let's Go Get Stoned	Ray Charles	146
Mack the Knife	Bobby Darin	152
Makin' Whoopee!	Eddie Cantor	159
Margaritaville	Jimmy Buffett	162
Misty	Johnny Mathis	166
Moondance	Van Morrison	169
Theme from New York, New York	Frank Sinatra	176
Night and Day	Ella Fitzgerald	181
Orange Colored Sky	Nat "King" Cole	186
The Pink Panther Theme	Henry Mancini	190
Raindrops Keep Fallin' on My Head	B.J. Thomas	194
Satin Doll	Duke Ellington	198
Save the Last Dance for Me	Michael Bublé	206
The Shadow of Your Smile	Tony Bennett	210
Theme from A Summer Place	Max Steiner	214
Summer Wind	Frank Sinatra	218
Take Five	Dave Brubeck Quartet	224
Taking a Chance on Love	Ella Fitzgerald	228
That's Amore	Dean Martin	232
There Will Never Be Another You	Rosemary Clooney	240
They Can't Take That Away from Me	Frank Sinatra	236
This Masquerade	George Benson	201
Walkin' My Baby Back Home	Nat "King" Cole	243
When I Fall in Love	Nat "King" Cole	246
Worrisome Heart	Melody Gardot	249
You Don't Know Me	Michael Bublé	254

AT LAST

Lyrics by
MACK GORDON

Music by
HARRY WARREN

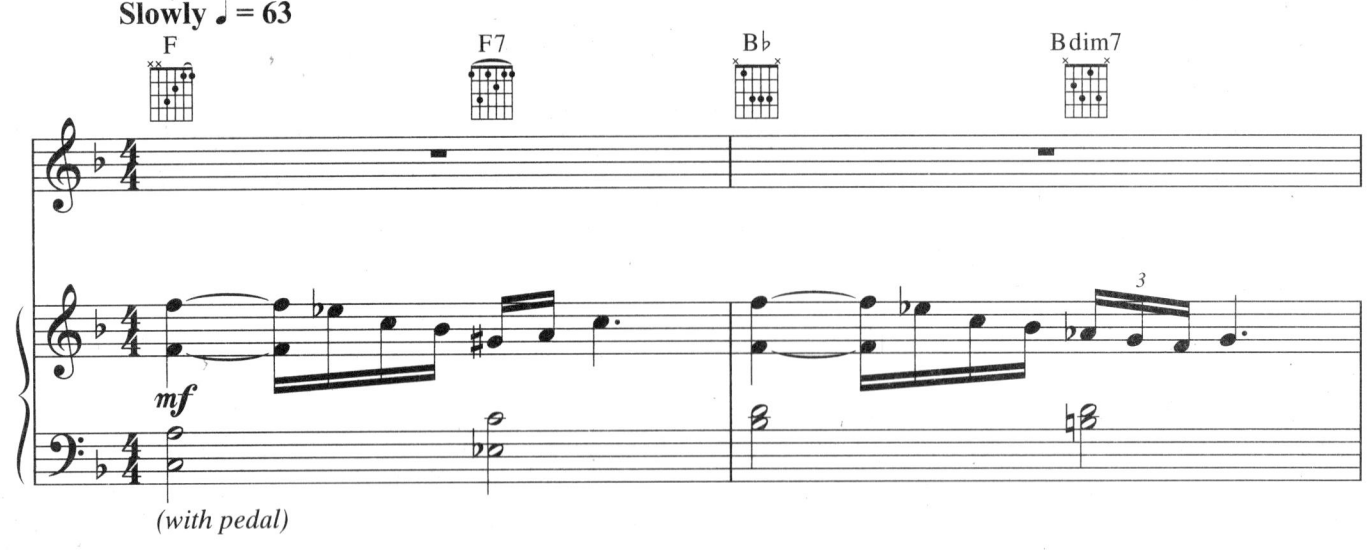

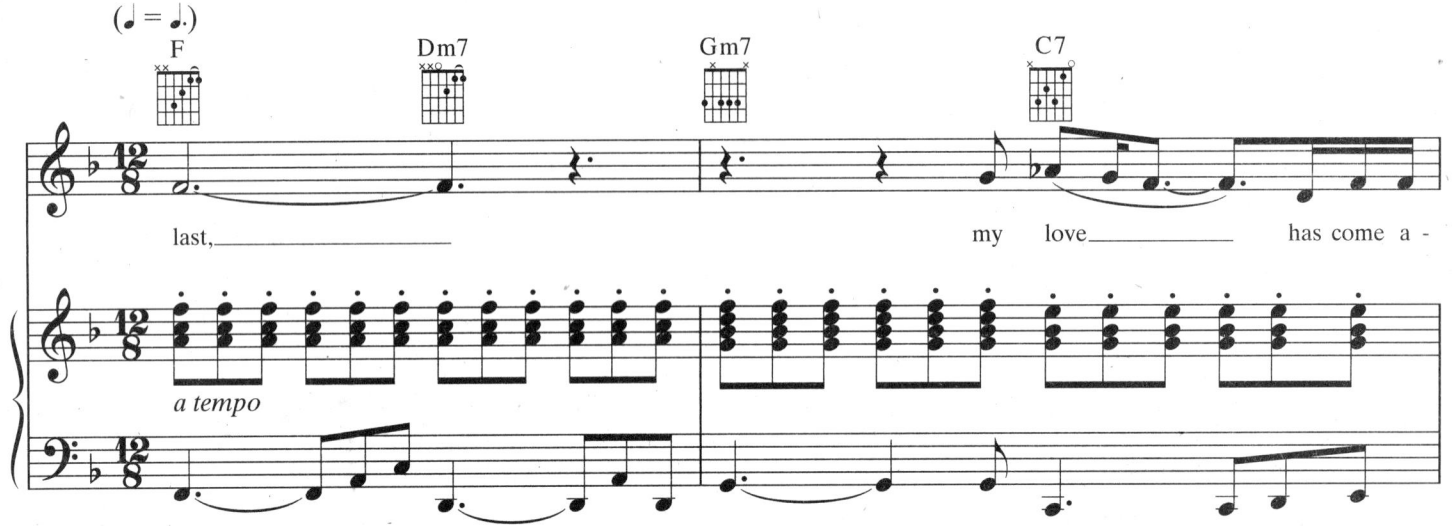

© 1942 (Renewed) TWENTIETH CENTURY MUSIC CORPORATION
All Rights Controlled by Emi Feist Catalog Inc. (Publishing) and ALFRED MUSIC PUBLISHING CO., INC. (Print)
All Rights Reserved

BLUEBERRY HILL

**Words and Music by
AL LEWIS, VINCENT ROSE
and LARRY STOCK**

Moderately ♩. = 92

Verse 1:

* Original recording in the key of B.

Blueberry Hill - 5 - 1

© 1940 (Renewed) CHAPPELL & CO., INC., LARRY STOCK MUSIC CO. (c/o LARRY SPIER MUSIC, LLC) and SOVEREIGN MUSIC CO.
All Rights Reserved

COME RAIN OR COME SHINE

Lyrics by
JOHNNY MERCER

Music by
HAROLD ARLEN

Freely

mf espressivo

rit.

Slowly and very tenderly

p a tempo

I'm gon-na love you like no-bod-y's loved you, come rain or come shine. High as a moun-tain and

Come Rain or Come Shine - 4 - 1

© 1946 (Renewed) CHAPPELL & CO., INC.
All Rights for the Extended Renewal Term in the U.S. Assigned to THE JOHNNY MERCER FOUNDATION and SA MUSIC
All Rights for THE JOHNNY MERCER FOUNDATION Administered by WB MUSIC CORP.
All Rights Reserved

C7 F7 G♭ Cm7 F7
deep as a riv - er, come rain or come shine.
ten.
B♭m Fm Gm7(♭5)
I guess when you met me, it was just one of those
molto espr.
C7(♭5) Fm6 Cm7(♭5)
things. But don't ev - er bet me, 'cause I'm
F♯dim7 Fdim7 C7 C7(♭9) Cdim7 G7 G7(♭5) C9
gon - na be true if you let me.
mf
dim.
rit.

You're gonna love me like nobody's loved me, come rain or come shine. Happy together, unhappy together, and won't it be fine? Days may be cloudy or sunny, we're in or we're out of the

Gm6
Dm7
G7
G
E7(♭5)
A
mon - ey, but I'm with you al - ways. I'm with you rain or
a tempo
f
1.
D7
G7
C7
C7(♭9)
2.
D7
shine!
shine!
rit. e dim.
p dim e rall
G7
C7
D
pp
(♭)

DAYS OF WINE AND ROSES

Words by
JOHNNY MERCER

Music by
HENRY MANCINI

Moderate ballad

Refrain:

The days ____ of wine and ros - es ____ laugh and run a - way ____ like a child at play, ____ through the mead - ow - land to - ward a clos - ing door, a door marked "Nev - er - more," that

Days of Wine and Roses - 2 - 1

© 1962 (Renewed) WB MUSIC CORP. and THE JOHNNY MERCER FOUNDATION
All Rights Administered by WB MUSIC CORP.
All Rights Reserved

Dm7(♭5) G9 Gm7 C7 F Cm6/E♭
was - n't there be - fore. The lone - ly night dis -
D7(♭9 ♭5) D9 Gm B♭m
clos - es just a pass - ing breeze filled with mem - o - ries
Am Dm Dm7/C Bm7(♭5) B♭9
of the gold - en smile that in - tro - duced me to the
Am Dm Gm7 1. F Fdim7 Gm7 C7 2. F Gm7 F
days of wine and ros - es and you. The you.
rall.

DESPERADO

Words and Music by
DON HENLEY and GLENN FREY

Slowly ♩ = 72

do, why don't you come to your senses? You been out ridin' fences for so long now. Oh, you're a

© 1973 (Renewed) CASS COUNTY MUSIC and RED CLOUD MUSIC
All Print Rights Administered by WARNER-TAMERLANE PUBLISHING CORP.
All Rights Reserved

G G7 C Cm6
hard one, I know that you got your rea - sons, these
G/D G+/D♯ Em A7 D7 G D/F♯
things that are pleas - in' you can hurt you some - how. Don't you
cresc.
Em Bm7 C G
draw the queen of dia - monds, boy, she'll beat you if she's a - ble. You know the
mf
Em C G D/F♯
queen of hearts is al - ways your best bet. Now it

Em7
Bm7
C
G
seems to me some fine things have been laid up - on your ta - ble, but you
Em
A7
Am7/D
D
on - ly want the ones that you can't get. Des - per - a -
poco rit. decresc.
G
G7
C
G/B
Am7
do, oh, you ain't get - tin' no young - er, your
a tempo
G
D/F♯
Em
A7
D7
pain and your hun - ger, they're driv - in' you home. And
3

freedom, oh, freedom, well, that's just some people talkin'. Your prison is walkin' through this world all alone. Don't your feet get cold in the winter-time? The sky won't snow and the sun won't shine. It's hard to tell the night-time from the day. You're

losin' all your highs and lows. Ain't it funny how the feeling goes away? Desperado, why don't you come to your senses? Come down from your fences, open the gate. It may be rainin', but there's a rain-bow a-bove you. You bet-ter let some-bod-y love you,

you___ bet-ter let some-bod-y love___ you___ be-

fore it's too___ late.

DON'T GET AROUND MUCH ANYMORE

Lyrics by
BOB RUSSELL

Music by
DUKE ELLINGTON

When I'm not play-ing sol-i-taire, I take a book down from the shelf. And

Don't Get Around Much Anymore - 4 - 1

© 1942 (Renewed) MUSIC SALES CORP. and SONY/ATV MUSIC PUBLISHING LLC,
8 Music Square West, Nashville, TN 37203
All Rights Reserved   Used by Permission

what, with pro - grams on the air,____ I keep pret - ty much__ to my -

Refrain:

self. Missed the Sat - ur - day dance, heard they crowd - ed the floor. Could - n't bear it with - out____ you.____ Don't get a - round much an - y - more. Thought I'd vis - it the *club, got as far as the door. They'd have asked me about you. Don't get around much anymore. Darling, I guess my mind's more at ease. But nevertheless,*

F♯m7(♭5)
B7
Em
B
G7
N.C.
why stir up mem - o - ries? Been in - vit - ed on
C6
A9
dates. Might have gone, but what for?
Am7
D7
G7
Aw - f'lly dif - f'rent with - out you. Don't get a - round much an - y -
1.
C6
N.C.
more. Missed the Sat - ur - day
2.
C6
more.
mf
p

DREAM A LITTLE DREAM OF ME

Lyrics by
GUS KAHN

Music by
FABIAN ANDRE and WILBUR SCHWANDT

Moderately

© 1931 (Renewed) GILBERT KEYES MUSIC, WORDS AND MUSIC, INC., DON SWAN PUBLICATIONS and ESSEX MUSIC, INC.
All Rights for GILBERT KEYES MUSIC Administered by WB MUSIC CORP.
All Rights Reserved

G Eb7 D7 G
Say "night - ie - night" and kiss me. Just hold me tight and
E7 Bm7(b5) E7 Am Am7 Am7(b5)
tell me you'll miss me. While I'm a - lone and blue as can be,
G Cm7 D7 G Am/G G Bb7 Eb Eb6
dream a lit - tle dream of me. Stars fad - ing, but
Bb7 Eb Eb6 Bb7 Bbdim7 Bb7 Eb Eb6
I lin - ger on, dear, still crav - ing your kiss; I'm long - ing to

B♭7 E♭ D D7sus D7
lin - ger till dawn, dear, just say - ing this:
G E♭7 D7 G
Sweet dreams till sun-beams find you, sweet dreams that leave all
E7 Bm7(♭5) E7 Am Am7 Am7(♭5)
wor - ries be - hind you, but in your dreams, what - ev - er they be,
1. 2.
G Cm7 D7 G E♭7 D7 G
dream a lit - tle dream of me. me.

ESCAPE
(The Piña Colada Song)

Words and Music by
RUPERT HOLMES

Moderately fast ♩ = 138

C
Em7(♭5)
F
Fmaj7/A
G7
F
Dm/G
like a worn - out re - cord - ing
of a fa - vor - ite song.
but me and my old la - dy
have fall - en in - to the same
I knew her smile in an in - stant.
I knew the curve of her face.
C
Cmaj7/E
Dm7
C
Em7(♭5)
F
Fmaj7/A
G7
old dull rou - tine.
So while she lay there sleep - ing,
So I wrote to the pa - per,
It was my own love - ly la - dy,
F
Dm/G
C
Cmaj7/E
Dm7
C
Em7(♭5)
I read the pa - per in bed,
took out a per - son - al ad.
and she said, "Oh, it's you."
and in the per - son - al col -
And though I'm no - bod - y's po -
Then we laughed for a mo -

umns, there was this let-ter I read:
et, I thought it was-n't half bad:
ment, and I said, "I nev-er knew

%% Chorus:

"If you like pi-ña co-la-das and get-ting caught in the
"Yes, I like pi-ña co-la-das and get-ting caught in the
that you like pi-ña co-la-das, get-ting caught in the

rain,
rain. if you're not in-to yo-ga,
rain, I'm not much in-to health food;
and the feel of the o-cean

Escape - 5 - 3

if you have half a brain,　　　　　　　　　　if you like mak-ing love at
I am in - to cham - pagne.
and the taste of cham - pagne.　　　　　　　If you'd like mak-ing love at

mid - night___　　　　in the dunes　on the Cape,　and cut through all　this red tape,
mor - row noon___
mid - night___　　　　in the dunes　on the Cape,

then I'm the love that you've looked for.　　　　　　　　　　Write to me and es-
at a bar called O' - Mal - ley's　　　　　　　　　　　　　where we'll plan our es-
you're the la - dy I've looked for.　　　　　　　　　　　　Come with me and es-

cape."
cape."
cape."

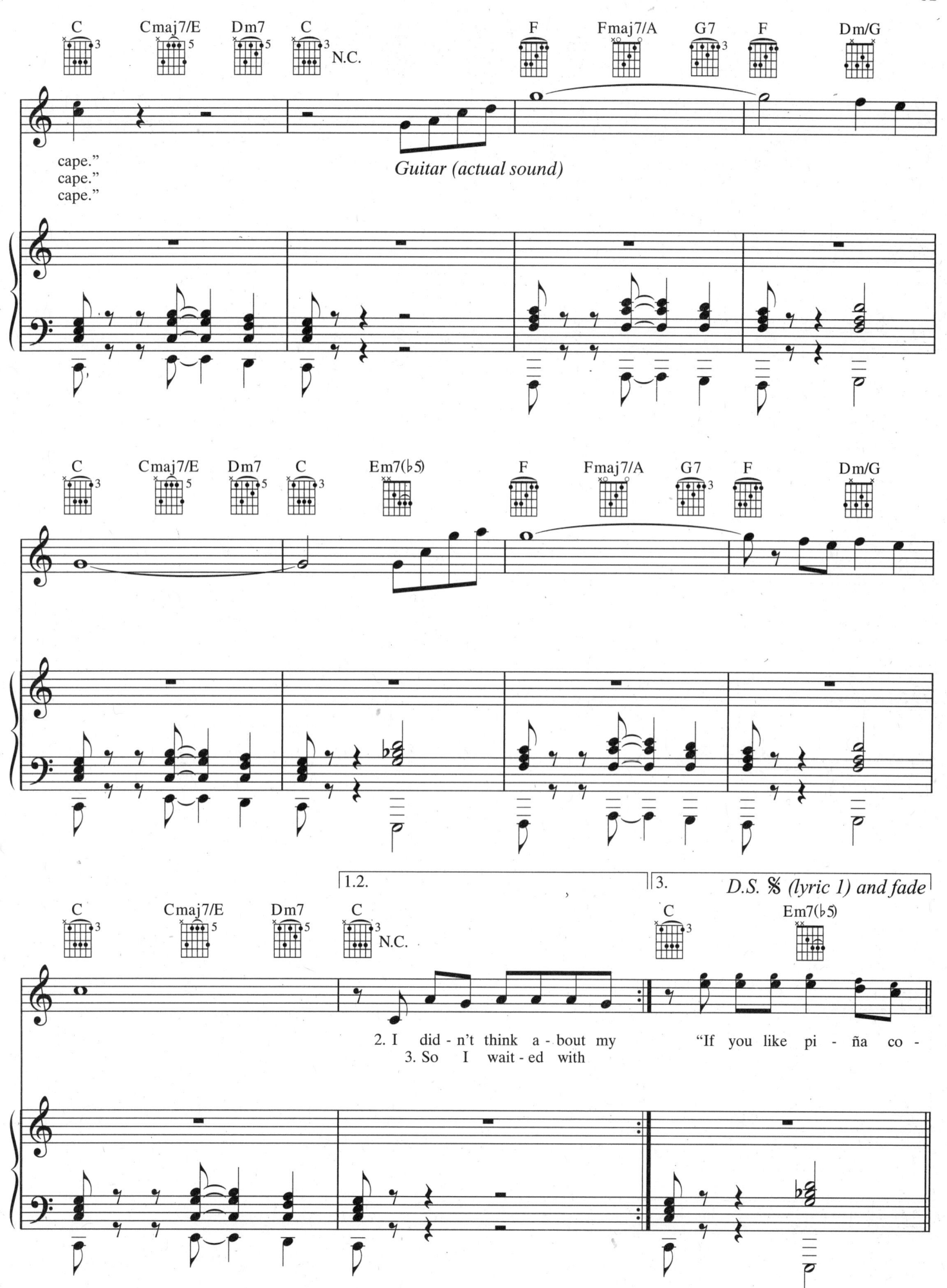

Guitar (actual sound)

2. I didn't think about my
3. So I waited with

"If you like piña co-

D.S. 𝄋 (lyric 1) and fade

FAITHFULLY

Words and Music by
JONATHAN CAIN

Slow rock ♩ = 66

1. High-way,
run into the midnight sun.
life under the big-top world.

© 1983 WEEDHIGH-NIGHTMARE MUSIC and LOVE BATCH MUSIC
All Rights for WEEDHIGH-NIGHTMARE MUSIC Administered by WIXEN MUSIC PUBLISHING INC.
All Rights Reserved

Wheels go 'round and 'round, you're on my mind.
We all need the clowns to make us smile.

Rest - less hearts sleep a -
Through space and time, al - ways an -

lone to - night, sendin' all my love a - long the
oth - er show. Won - d'ring where I am, lost with -

wire. They say that the road ain't no place to start a fam -
out you. And be - in' a - part ain't eas - y on this love

'ly.
af-fair. Right down the line it's been you and me.
Two strang-ers learn to fall in love a-

gain.
And lov-in' a mu-sic man ain't al-ways what it's
I get the joy of re-dis-

s'pposed to be.
cov-'ring you. Oh, girl, you stand by

me. I'm for-ev-er yours,

faith - ful - ly.

2. Cir - cus

Oh, oh,

oh.

Faithfully - 4 - 4

HIT THE ROAD JACK

Words and Music by
PERCY MAYFIELD

Moderately fast ♩ = 172

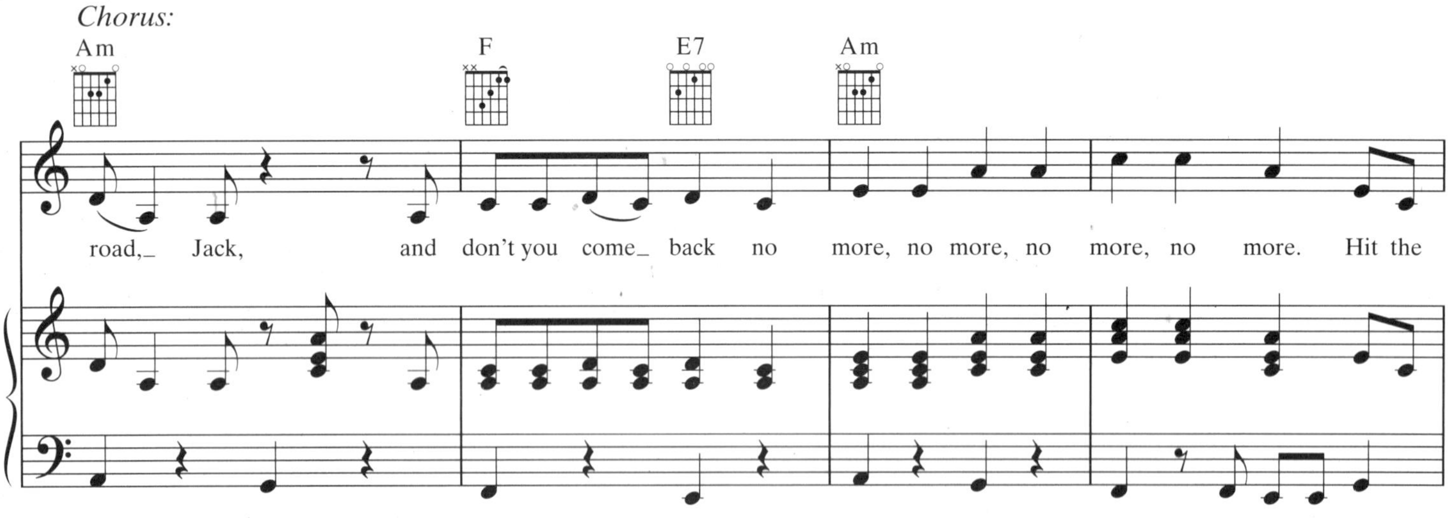

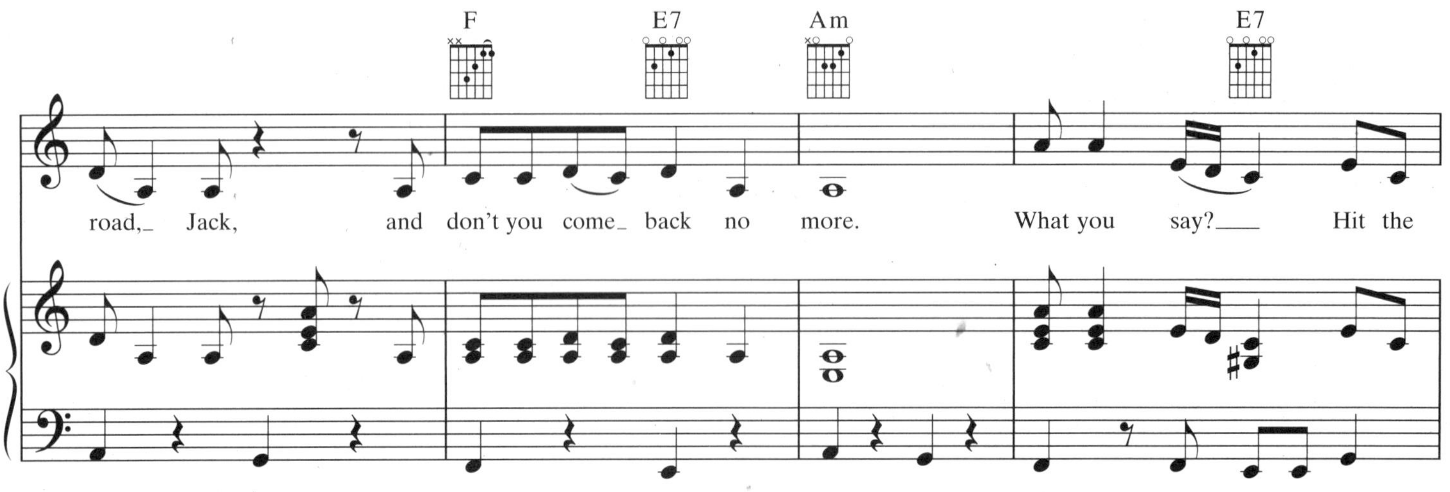

*Original recording in A♭ minor.

© 1961 (Renewed) TANGERINE MUSIC CORP.
All Rights Reserved Used by Permission

Am F E7 Am F E7
road,_ Jack, and don't you come_ back no more, no more, no more, no more. Hit the
F E7 Am
road,_ Jack, and don't you come_ back no more. 1. Whoa,
Verse 1:
F E7 Am F E7
wom-an, oh, wom-an, don't treat me so__ mean. You're the mean-est old wom-an that I've ev - er seen._ I
Am E7 Am
guess if__ you said so, I'd have to pack my things_ and go. That's right! Hit the

Chorus:
F E7 Am F E7
road,_ Jack, and don't you come_ back no more, no more, no more, no more. Hit the
Am F E7 Am E7
road,_ Jack, and don't you come_ back no more. What you say?__ Hit the
Am F E7 Am F E7
road,_ Jack, and don't you come_ back no more, no more, no more, no more. Hit the
Am F E7 Am
road,_ Jack, and don't you come_ back no more. 2. Now,

Verse 2:
F E7 Am F E7
ba - by, lis - ten, ba - by, don't ya treat me this a - way, 'cause I'll be back on my feet some - day. Don't
Am F E7 Am F E7
care if you do, 'cause it's un - der - stood; you ain't got no mon - ey, you just ain't no good. Well, I
Am E7 Am
guess if a - you say so, I'll have to pack my things and go. That's right! Hit the
Chorus:
F E7 Am F E7
road, Jack, and don't you come back no more, no more, no more, no more. Hit the

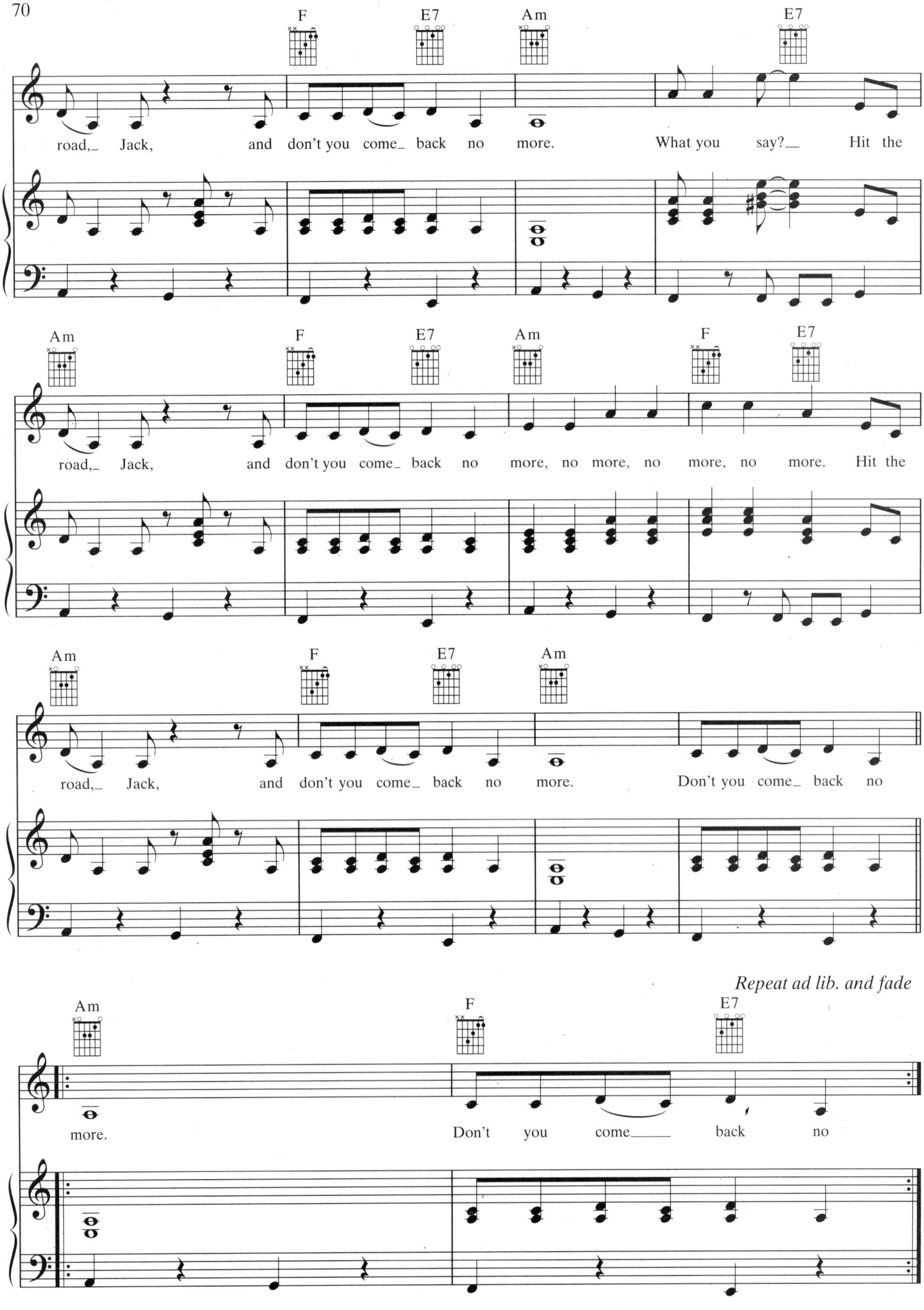

HOW DEEP IS YOUR LOVE

Words and Music by
BARRY GIBB, MAURICE GIBB
and ROBIN GIBB

Fm7/B♭
E♭
Gm7
Cm7
And the mo - ment that you wan-der far from me, I wan-na
You're the light in my deep-est, dark - est hour. You're my
Na na na na na na na na na na na na na
Fm7
Fm7/B♭
A♭maj7
feel you in my arms a - gain. And you come to me on a sum -
Sav - iour when I fall. And you may not think I care
na na na na na na. And you come to me on a sum -
Gm7
Fm7
mer breeze, keep me warm in your love, then you soft -
for you, when you know down in - side that I real -
mer breeze, keep me warm in your love then you soft -
D♭9
Gm7
A♭maj7/B♭
ly leave.
ly do.
ly leave.
And it's me you need to show;
How deep
how deep is your love.

Chorus:
E♭
E♭maj7
A♭maj7
is your love, how deep is your love? I real - ly mean to learn.
A♭m6
E♭
B♭m/A♭
'Cause we're liv - ing in a world of fools, break - ing us
C7
Fm7
1.2.
A♭m6
down when they all should let us be. We be - long to you and me.
3.
A♭m6
E♭
Gm7
A♭maj7/B♭
D.S. and fade
to you and me. Na na na na na. How deep

HOME

Words and Music by
MICHAEL BUBLÉ, ALAN CHANG
and AMY FOSTER

Moderately slow ♩ = 72

Verse:
1. An-oth-er sum-mer day has come and gone a-way in Par-is and Rome,_ but I wan-na go home._

May be sur-round-ed by a mil-lion peo-ple, I still feel all a-lone,_ just wan-na go home._ Oh, I miss you, you know. I've been keep-ing all_ the let-ters_ that I wrote to you, each one a line_
feel just like_ I'm liv-ing_ some-one els-e's life. It's like I just stepped_

or two,— "I'm fine, ba-by. How are you?"— Well, I would
out-side,— when ev-'ry-thing was go-ing right.— And I

send them, but— I know— that it's— just not e-nough. My words were cold—
know just why— you could-n't come— a-long with me. This was not—

— and flat,— and you de-serve more———— than that.
— your dream,— but you al-ways be-lieved———— in me.

An-oth-er ae-ro-plane, an-oth-er sun-ny place. I'm luck-y, I know,— but I wan-na go home.—
An-oth-er win-ter day has come and gone a-way in ei-ther Par-is or Rome,— and I wan-na go home.—

77

Cmaj7 | D *To Coda* ✛ G | Bm/D D

I've got to go home. Let me go home.
Let me go

Chorus:
G | D6 | Em7 | Bm7

I'm just too

Cmaj9 | D G | Bm/D D

far from where you are, I wan-na come home.

G | D/F# | Em7 | D(4)

Home - 6 - 4

And I home. And I'm sur-round-ed by a mil-lion peo-ple, I, I still feel a-lone,__ oh, let__ me go home.__ Oh, I miss you, you know.

Chorus:
Let me go home.__

79

Lyrics:
I've had my run, and, baby, I'm done. I've gotta go home. Let me go home. It'll be alright, I'll be home tonight. I'm coming back home.

HOW DO YOU KEEP THE MUSIC PLAYING?

Lyrics by
ALAN and MARILYN BERGMAN

Music by
MICHEL LEGRAND

Moderate ballad

How do you keep the music playing?
How do you make it last?
How do you keep the song from fading too fast?

How Do You Keep the Music Playing? - 5 - 1

© 1982 WB MUSIC CORP.
All Rights Reserved

Gm7
C7sus
C7
Fmaj7
How do you lose your-self to some - one and nev-er lose your
Dm7
Em7(♭5)
A7sus
A7
way? How do you not run out of new things to
Dm
Dm7(♭5)
G7(♭9)
Cm7
say? And since we know we're al - ways
F7sus
F7
B♭maj7
Gm7
chang - ing, how can it be the same?

And tell me how, year after year, you're sure your heart will fall a-part___ each time you hear {his/her} name?___ I know the way I feel for you, it's now or nev-er. The

Second time only
How do you keep the mu-sic play-ing? How do you make it

[Bbmaj7] more I love, the more that I'm a-fraid [Em7(b5)] that [A7sus] in your eyes I may not see for-[A7]last? How do you keep the song from fad-ing,

[Dm] ev-er [Dm7(b5)] for-ev-er. [G7(b9)] [Cm7] If we can be the best of keep the song from fad-ing too fast?

[F7sus] lov-[F7]ers, [Bbmaj7] yet be the best of [Gm7] friends,

E♭maj7
Dm7
Dm7/G
G7(♭9)
Cm9
if we can try with ev - 'ry day to make it bet - ter as it grows,
Cm7(♭5)
F7sus
F7
with an - y luck, then I sup - pose the mu - sic nev - er
1.
2.
E♭/B♭
B♭
E♭/B♭
B♭
ends. I ends.

HUMAN NATURE

Words and Music by
JOHN BETTIS and STEVE PORCARO

G
A
G
A
time, the cit - y winks a sleep - less eye.
G
A
G
Hear her voice shake my win -
A
G
F♯m7
Em7
Asus4
dow: sweet, se - duc - ing sighs.
G
A
G
A
Get me out in - to the night -
Reach - ing out to touch a stran -
Look - ing out a - cross the morn -

time.
Four walls won't hold me tonight.
ger, electric eyes are ev-'ry-where.
ing, the city's heart begins to beat.

If this town is just an ap-
See that girl? She knows I'm watch-
Reach-ing out, I touch her shoul-

ple, then let me take a bite.
ing. She likes the way I stare.
der. I'm dreaming of the street.

A G A D D/C♯
If they_ say, "Why, why?" tell 'em that_ it's hu -
Bm7 A G F♯m7 Em7
man na - ture. Why, why does he do me that way?
Bm G A D D/C♯
If they_ say, "Why, why?" tell 'em that_ it's hu -
Bm7 A G F♯m7
To Coda
man na - ture. Why, why does he

1.
Em7
A
2.
Em7
do me that way?
do me that way?
Bm
Em7
Bm
I like liv - in' this way.
I like
Em7
Bm
Em9
lov - in' this way.
Gmaj7/A
2 fr.
G(addA)
A

Fmaj7
Em7
G(addA)
A
Fmaj7
Em7
D. S. 𝄋 al Coda ⊕
Coda ⊕
Em9
do me that way?
Gmaj7/A
2 fr.
G(addA)
A
I like liv-in' this way._
Fmaj7
Em7

G(addA)
A
Fmaj7
Em7
B♭maj7
Am7
Fmaj7
Em7
B♭maj7
Repeat and fade
B♭maj7

I GET A KICK OUT OF YOU

Words and Music by
COLE PORTER

Moderately

Verse:

My story is much too sad to be told, but prac-ti-c'lly ev-'ry-thing leaves me to-tal-ly cold. The on-ly ex-cep-tion I know is the case when I'm out on a

I Get a Kick Out of You - 5 - 1

© 1934 (Renewed) WB MUSIC CORP.
All Rights Reserved

qui - et spree___ fight-ing vain - ly the old en - nui,___ and I sud - den - ly
turn and see___ your fab - u - lous face.

Refrain:

I get no kick from cham - pagne,___ mere al - co -
hol does-n't thrill me at all, so tell me why should it be true___

Gm7 Fm Bb7 Eb Gm
that I get a kick out of you?
Fm7 Bb7 Eb Gm Fm7
Some get a kick from co - caine,
I'm sure that
Bb7 Eb Gm Fm7 F7 Bb A Ab
if I took e - ven one sniff that would bore me ter - rif - i - c'lly
Eb Gm Fm7 Bb7 Eb
too.
Yet I get a kick out of you.

I get a kick ev-'ry time I see you're stand-ing there be-fore me. I get a kick tho' it's clear to me you ob-vious-ly don't a-dore me. I get no kick in a

plane, flying too high with some
{gal/guy} in the sky is my i-dea of noth-ing to
do. Yet I get a kick out of
you. you.

IT HAD TO BE YOU

Words by
GUS KAHN

Music by
ISHAM JONES

Moderately

It had to be you,_____ it had to be you._____ I wan-dered a-round____ and fi-nal-ly found____ the some-bod-y who_____ could make me be true,_

It Had to Be You - 3 - 1

© 1924 (Renewed) GILBERT KEYES MUSIC and THE BANTAM MUSIC PUBLISHING CO.
All Rights Administered by WB MUSIC CORP.
All Rights Reserved

could make me be blue, and e-ven be glad just to be sad think-ing of you. Some oth-ers I've seen might nev-er be mean, might nev-er be cross

It Had to Be You - 3 - 2

A7
or try to be boss, but they would-n't do.
Am Am7/G F♯dim7 D7
For no-bod-y else gave me a thrill. With all your faults,
G B7 Em B♭dim7 D7 B♭dim7 D7
I love you still. It had to be you, won-der-ful you, had to be you.
1.
G B♭dim7 Am7(♭5) D7 D+
It had to be you.
2.
G Cm6 G6

IF YOU DON'T KNOW ME BY NOW

Slow ballad, in six ♪ = 104

Words and Music by
KENNETH GAMBLE and LEON HUFF

(Bkgrd.) (If you don't know me by now, you will never, never, never know me. Ooh.)

Verse 1:
1. All the things that we've been through,

---
* Background vocals sung at pitch.

If You Don't Know Me by Now - 6 - 1

© 1973 (Renewed) WARNER-TAMERLANE PUBLISHING CORP. and MIJAC MUSIC (BMI)
All Rights Administered by WARNER-TAMERLANE PUBLISHING CORP.
All Rights Reserved

E♭
Cm7/F
F
Gm7
F7/A
you should un - der - stand me
like I un - der - stand you.
B♭
Dm7
Now, girl, I know the dif - f'rence
be - tween right and wrong.
E♭
Cm7/F
F
Gm7
F7/A
I ain't gon - na do noth - in'
to break up our hap - py home.
D♭
G♭maj7
Oh, don't get so ex - cit - ed
when I come home a lit - tle late at night,

E♭m7
Cm7/F
F
Gm7
F7/A
'cause we on - ly act like chil - dren when we ar - gue, fuss, and fight.
Chorus:
B♭
Dm7
If you don't know me,
(Bkgrd.) (If you don't know me by now, you will
E♭
E♭m6/G♭
No, you won't.
nev - er, nev - er, nev - er know me. Ooh.)
B♭
Dm7
(If you don't know me by now, you will

E♭
E♭m6/G♭
nev - er, nev - er, nev - er know me.
Ooh.)
Verse 2:
B♭
Dm7
2. We've all got our own fun - ny moods.
E♭
Cm7/F
F
Gm7
F7/A
I got mine; wom - an, you got yours too.
B♭
Dm7
Just trust in me like I trust in you.

As long as we've been to-geth-er, it should be so eas-y to do. just get your-self to-geth-er, or we might as well say good-bye. What good is a love af-fair when you can't see eye to eye?

Chorus:
(If you don't know me by now, If you don't know me, you will

If You Don't Know Me by Now - 6 - 5

E♭
E♭m6/G♭
B♭
No, you won't.
nev-er, nev-er, nev-er know_ me.
Ooh.
)
(If you don't know me by
Dm7
E♭
you
will
nev - er,
nev - er,
nev - er
know
me.
now,
you will
nev - er,
nev - er,
nev - er
know_
me.
E♭m6/G♭
B♭
Ooh.
)
(If you don't know me by
Dm7
E♭
E♭m6/G♭
Mm.
now,
you will
nev - er,
nev - er,
nev - er
know_
me.
Ooh.)

I'VE GOT A CRUSH ON YOU

Music and Lyrics by
GEORGE GERSHWIN
and IRA GERSHWIN

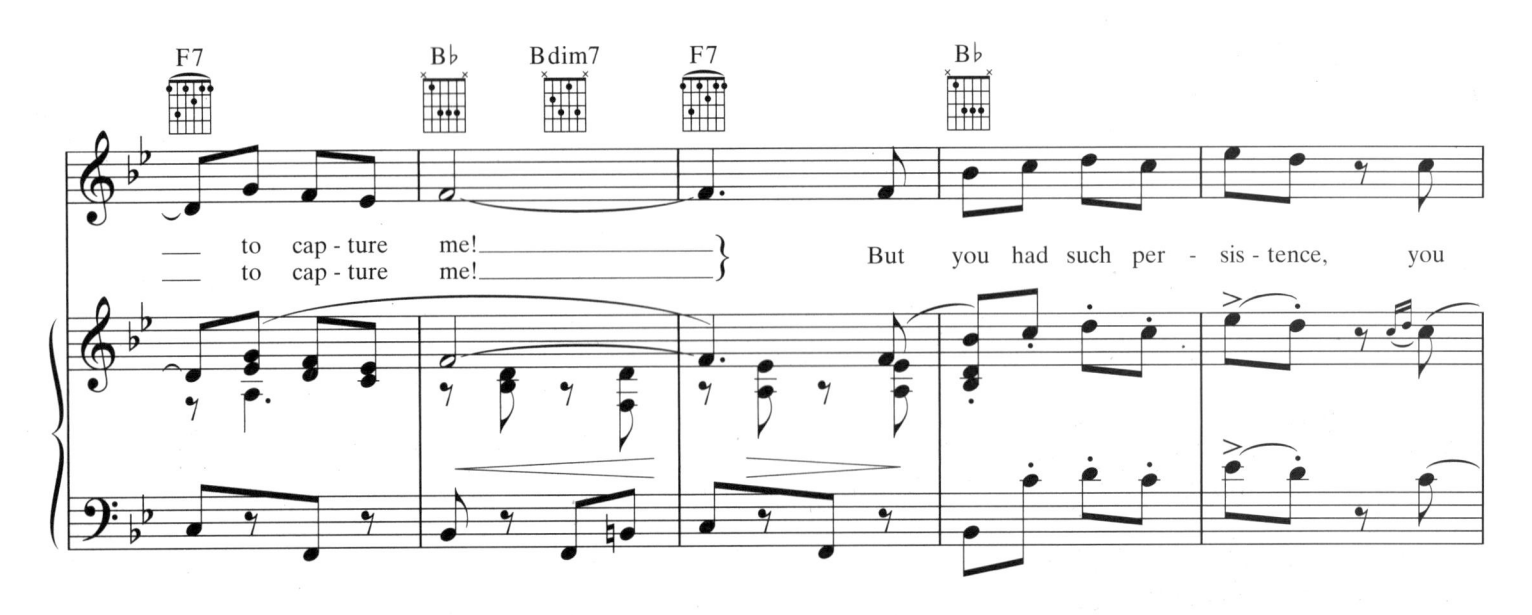

Allegretto giocoso

He: How
She: How

Verse:

glad the man-y mil-lions of An-na-belles and Lil-lians would be
glad a mil-lion lad-dies from mil-lion-aires to cad-dies would be

to cap-ture me! But you had such per-sis-tence, you
to cap-ture me!

I've Got a Crush on You - 4 - 1

© 1930 (Renewed) WB MUSIC CORP.
All Rights Reserved

wore down my re-sis-tance; I fell, and it was swell.

She: You're my big and brave and hand-some Ro-me-o. How I won you, I shall nev-er, nev-er know. *He:* It's not that you're at-trac-tive, but oh, my heart grew ac-tive when you came in-to view.

I've Got a Crush on You - 4 - 2

Moderately

Refrain:

He: I've got a crush on you, Sweet-ie Pie.
She: I've got a crush on you, Sweet-ie Pie.

All the day and night-time, hear me sigh. I nev-er had the least
All the day and night-time, hear me sigh. This is-n't just a flir -

no - tion that I could fall with so much e - mo - tion.
ta - tion: we're prov-ing that there's pre - des - ti - na - tion.

I've Got a Crush on You - 4 - 3

Could you coo,_____ could you care_____ for a cun-ning cot-tage
I could coo,_____ I could care_____ for that cun-ning cot-tage

we could share?___ The world will par - don my mush, 'cause I've got a
we could share.___ Your mush I nev - er shall shush, 'cause I've got a

crush, my ba - by, on you._____ I've got a you._____
crush, my ba - by, on

I've Got a Crush on You - 4 - 4

I'VE GOT YOU UNDER MY SKIN

Words and Music by
COLE PORTER

Allegretto sostenuto

Refrain:

I've got you _____ un-der my skin, _____ I've got you _____

deep in the heart of me, so deep in my heart, you're really a part of me. I've got you under my skin. I tried so

B♭7
E♭maj7
E♭6
not to give in,
I
Fm7(♭5)
B♭7sus(♭9)
B♭7
D
E♭maj7
said to my-self, "This af - fair
nev - er will go so well."
E♭6
Dm7
F/G
G7
But
why should I try to re - sist
when, dar - ling, I
mf
Cdim7
C
A♭6
know so well
I've got you
marcato

B♭7(♭9)
E♭maj7
E♭6
under my skin?
I'd
Fm7/E♭
B♭7/E♭
E♭
sac - ri - fice an - y - thing, come what might, for the sake of hav - ing you
poco a poco cresc. ed appassionato
E♭7
Fm/E♭
Fm7(♭5)/E♭
near, in spite of a warn - ing voice that comes in the night and re -
subito p
E♭
B♭7
Cm
peats and re - peats in my ear, "Don't you know, lit - tle fool,
molto cresc.
f molto espressivo

you never can win, use your mentality, wake up to reality." But each time I do, just the thought of you makes me stop before I begin, 'cause I've

I've Got You Under My Skin - 6 - 5

Fm
B♭7(♭9)
E♭
got you under my skin.
a tempo
rit.
pp
a tempo
1.
2.
E♭maj7
E♭6
Fm7
B♭7
E♭
I've
poco rit.
poco rall.
B♭7
E♭
più rall.
r.h.
morendo
ppp
8vb

KILLING ME SOFTLY WITH HIS SONG

Words and Music by
CHARLES FOX and NORMAN GIMBEL

Moderately ♩ = 112

Chorus:

Strum-ming my pain with his fin - gers, sing-ing my life with his words.

Kill-ing me soft - ly with his song, kill-ing me soft-ly with his song, tell-ing my whole life with his

Killing Me Softly With His Song - 6 - 1

© 1972 (Renewed) RODALI MUSIC and GIMBEL MUSIC GROUP
All Rights for RODALI MUSIC Administered by WARNER-TAMERLANE PUBLISHING CORP.
All Rights Reserved

D♭
G♭maj7(♯11)
F
words, kill - ing me soft - ly with his song.
A little faster ♩ = 120
E♭7sus
E♭7
E♭7sus
E♭7
E♭7sus
E♭7
E♭7sus
E♭7
Verse:
B♭m7
E♭7
1. I heard he sang a good song,
2. I felt all flushed with fe - ver,
3. He sang as if he knew me,

I heard he had a style.
em - bar - rassed by the crowd.
in all my dark de - spair.
And so I came
I felt he found
And then he looked

to see him, to lis - ten for a while.
my let - ters and read each one out loud.
right through me, as if I was - n't there.

And there he was, this young boy,
I prayed that he would fin - ish,
And he just kept on sing - ing,
a strang - er to
but he just kept
sing - ing clear

Chorus:
my eyes...
right on...
and strong...
Strum - ming my pain with his fin - gers,

Killing Me Softly With His Song - 6 - 3

E♭
A♭
Fm
sing-ing my life with his words.
Kill-ing me soft - ly with his
B♭/D
E♭
D♭
A♭
song, kill-ing me soft - ly with his song, tell-ing my whole life with his
To Coda
D♭
G♭maj7(♯11)
F
words, kill-ing me soft - ly with his song.
1.2.
3.
Bridge:
Fm
B♭m7
Oh,

120

La la la la la, oh, oh, la, softly. He was

Chorus:
Fm7
B♭m7/F
E♭/B♭
strum-ming my pain,
yeah, he was sing - ing my life.
A♭
Fm
B♭/D
Kill - ing me soft - ly with his song, kill - ing me soft -
E♭
D♭
A♭
D♭
ly with his song, tell - ing my whole life with his words, kill - ing
G♭maj7(♯11)
F
me soft - ly with his song.

JUST ONE OF THOSE THINGS

Words and Music by
COLE PORTER

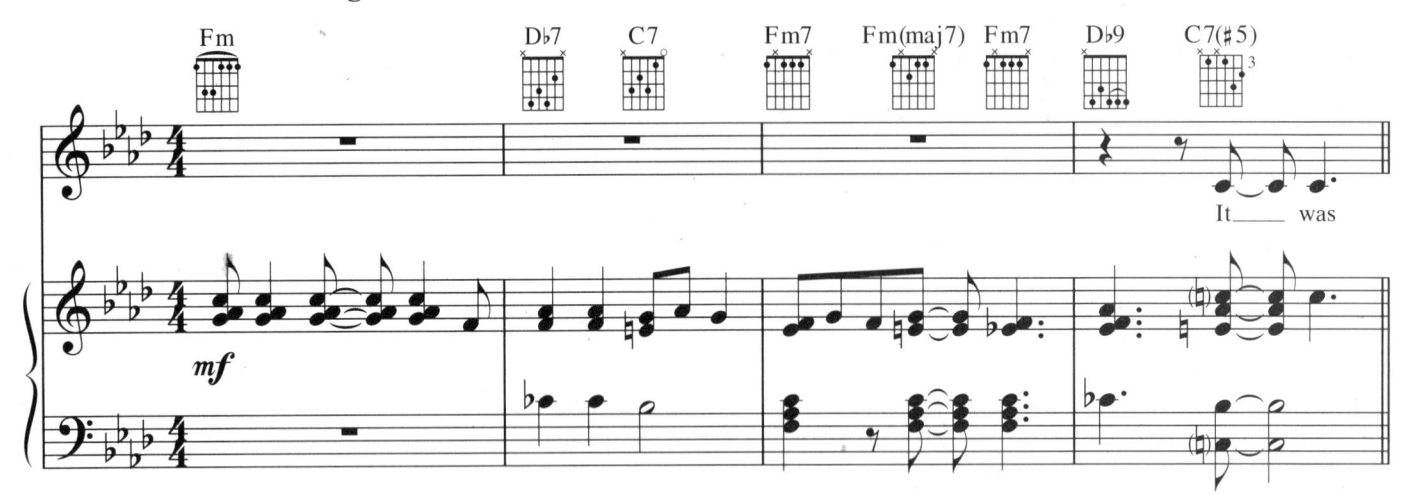

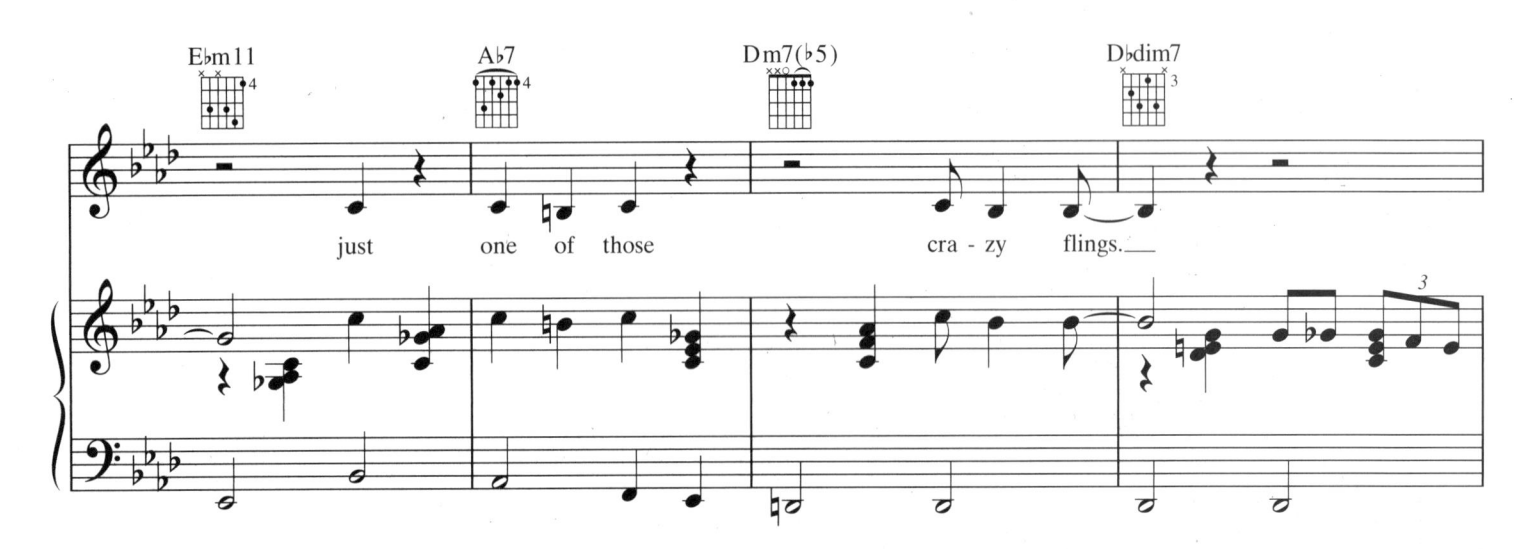

Medium swing ♩ = 138

It___ was just one of those things, just one of those cra-zy flings.___

Cm7
Fm7
B♭m7
E♭7
One of those bells that now and then rings,
A♭maj7
F7/A
B♭m7
C7
Just one of those things. It was
Fm
C
just one of those nights,
E♭m11
A♭7
Dm7(♭5)
D♭dim7
just one of those fab - u - lous flights.

Cm7
Bdim7
B♭m7
E♭7
A trip to the moon on gos - sa - mer wings,
Cm7
Bdim7
B♭m7
D♭13
just one of those things. If we'd
G♭maj7
A♭m9
D♭7
thought a bit of the end of it when we
G♭maj7
B7
Fm7
B♭7
start - ed paint - ing the town, we'd have

Cm
Cm7/B♭
Am7(♭5)
A♭m(maj7)
A♭m7
been a - ware that our love af - fair was too
Gm7
G♭dim7
Fdim7
E13
C7(♯9)
hot not to cool down. So good -
Fm
C
bye, dear, and A - men.
E♭m11
A♭7
Dm7(♭5)
D♭dim7
Here's hop - ing we'll meet now and then, It was

Cm7
F7
B♭m11
great fun___ but it was just
1.
E♭13
A♭maj7
D♭13
Cm7
F7(♭9 ♯5)
B♭m7
F7
one of those things.__
Gm7
C7(♯5)
2.
E♭13
N.C. D♭maj7
It was one of those things.
Cm7
B7
B♭m7
A13
A♭maj13(♯11)
poco rit.

THE LADY IS A TRAMP

Words by
LORENZ HART

Music by
RICHARD RODGERS

Moderately (in two)

Bunny: I've wined and dined on mul-li-gan stew and nev-er wished for tur-key, as I hitched and hiked and drift-ed, too, from Maine to Al-bu-quer-que. A-las, I missed the Beaux Arts Ball and, what is twice as sad, I was nev-er at a par-ty where they hon-ored No-el Ca-'ad. But

© 1937 (Renewed) CHAPPELL & CO., INC.
Rights for the Extended Term of Copyright in the U.S. Controlled by WB MUSIC CORP. and WILLIAMSON MUSIC CO.
All Rights Reserved

social circles spin too fast for me. My hobohemia is the place to be.

1. I get too hungry for dinner at eight.
2. I go to Coney, the beach is divine.

I like the theatre, but never come late.
I go to ball games, the bleachers are fine.

I never bother with people I hate.
That's why the lady is a tramp!
I don't like crap games with barons and earls,
I won't go to Harlem in ermine and pearls,

I follow Winchell and read ev'ry line.
That's why the lady is a tramp!
I like a prize fight that isn't a fake.
I love the rowing in Central Park Lake.

The Lady Is a Tramp - 5 - 3

A Amaj7 A9 A9(♯5) D6 Dm Bm7(♭5)
won't dish the dirt with the rest of the girls.
I go to op - era and stay wide a - wake.
A/E A+/C♯ D6 E7 A E9(♯5) A
That's why the la - dy is a tramp! I like the
That's why the la - dy is a tramp! I like the
Dmaj7 E13 C♯m7 F♯m7
free, fresh wind in my hair,
green grass un - der my shoes.
Bm7 E7 A F♯7 B7 E7
life with-out care. I'm broke! It's oke!
What can I lose? I'm flat! That's that!
mf

Hate Cal - i - for - nia, it's cold and it's damp.
I'm all a - lone when I low - er my lamp.

1.
That's why the la - dy is a tramp.

2.
That's why the la - dy is a

tramp!

The Lady Is a Tramp - 5 - 5

LAURA

Lyrics by
JOHNNY MERCER

Music by
DAVID RAKSIN

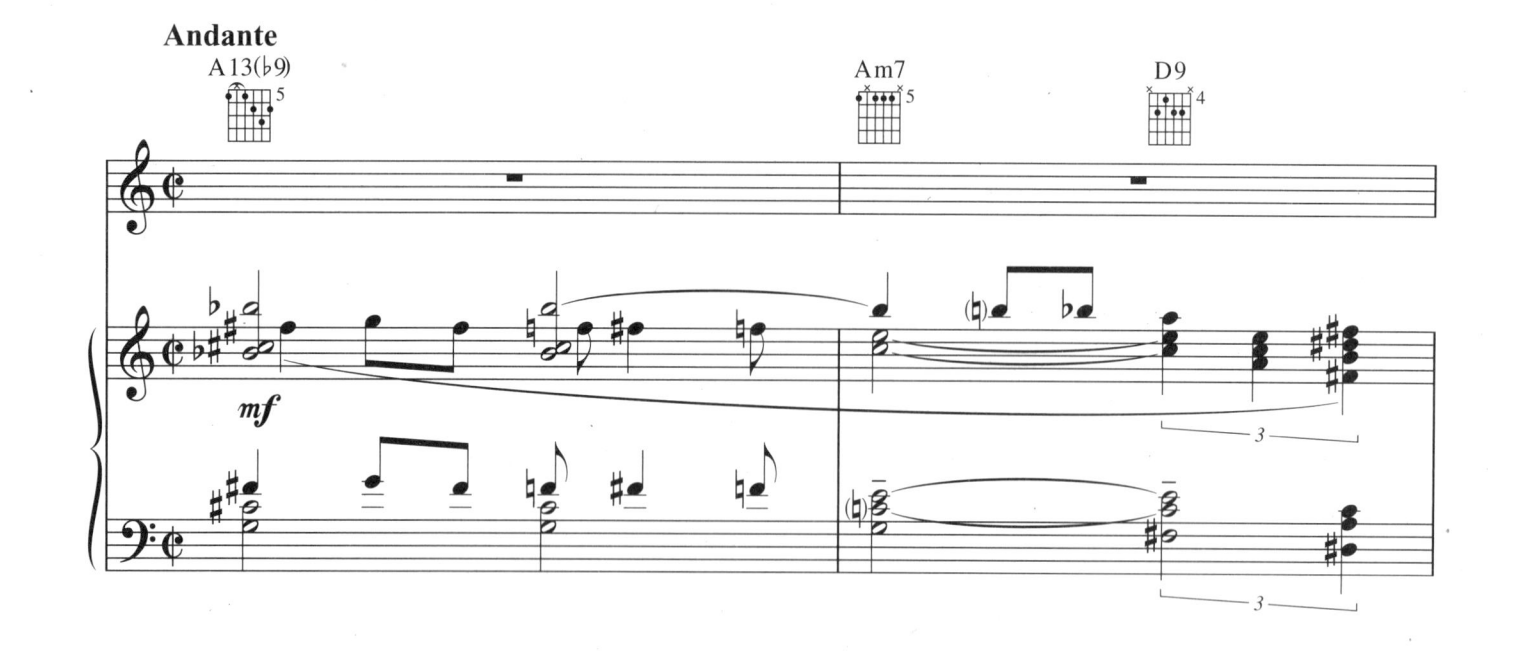

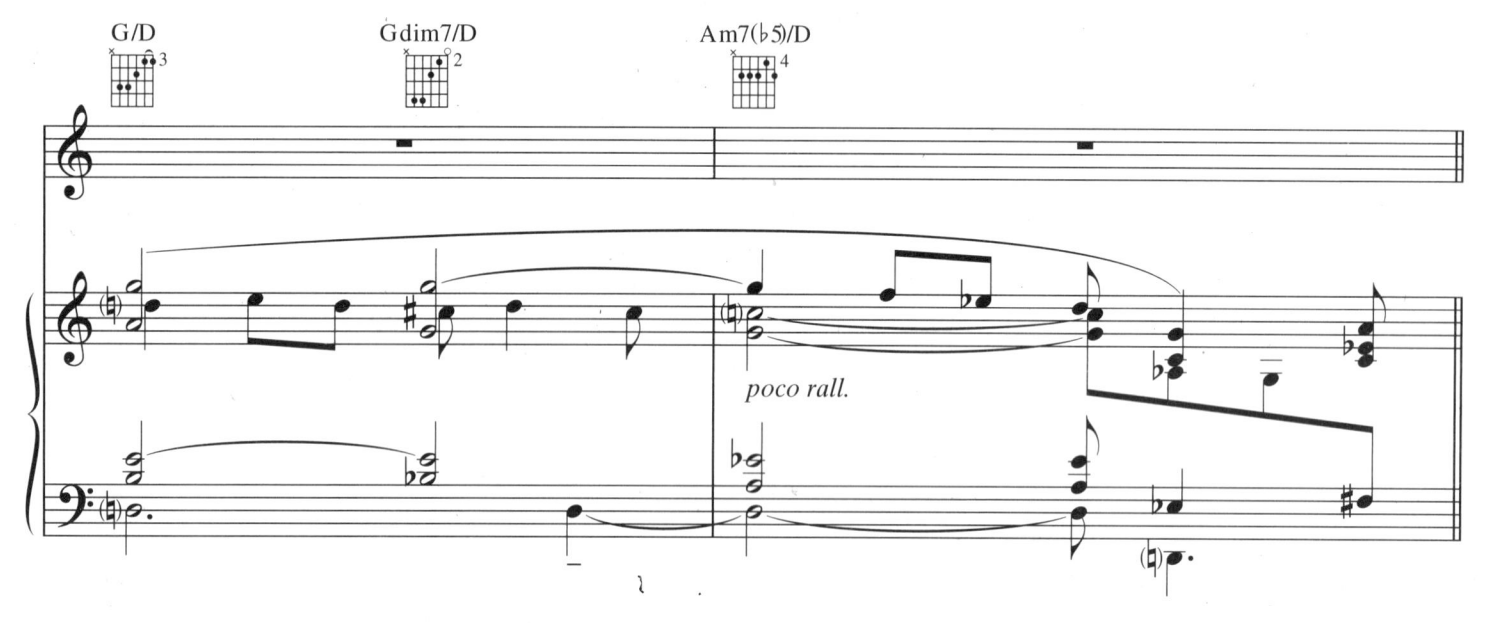

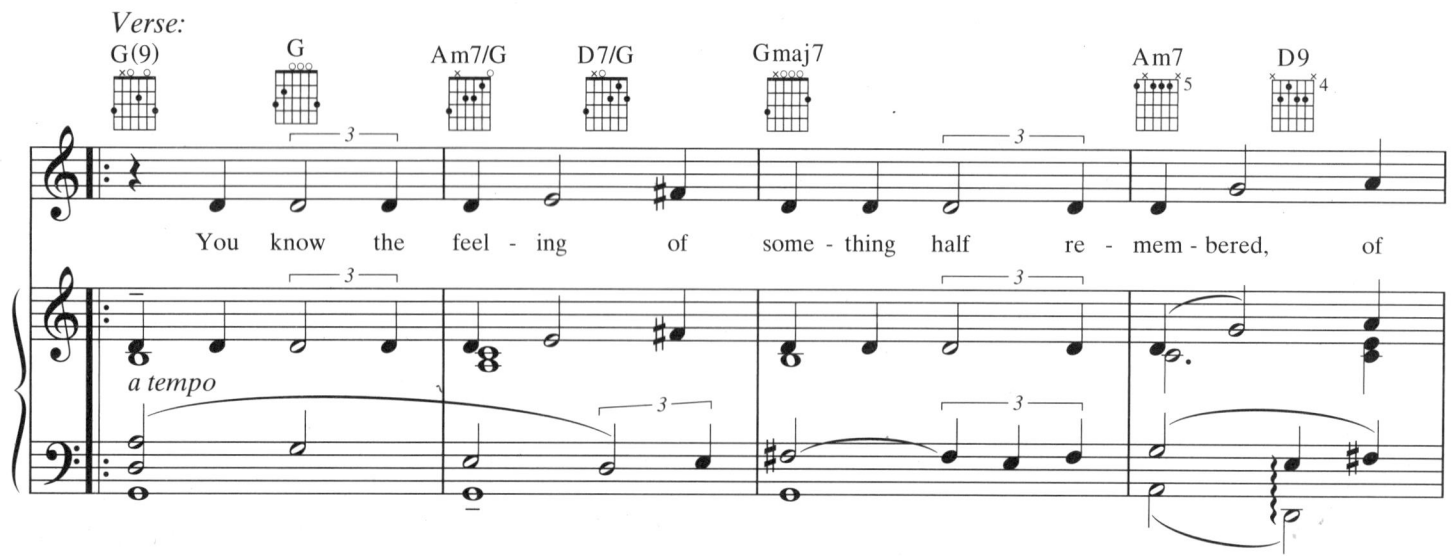

Verse: You know the feel-ing of some-thing half re-mem-bered, of somethnig that never happened. Yet you recall it well. You know the feeling of recognizing someone that you've never met, as far as you could tell; well:

Moderato
Chorus:
Am9
D7(♭9 ♯5)
Gmaj9
G6
Lau - ra is the face in the mist - y light,
mf
Gm9
C7(♭9 ♯5)
Fmaj9
F6/9
foot - steps that you hear down the hall.
Fm7
B♭7sus
B♭7
E♭maj7
E♭6
The laugh that floats on a sum - mer night that you can

never quite recall. And you see Laura on the train that is passing through. Those eyes, how familiar they seem.

Lyrics:

She gave your very first kiss to you, that was Laura, but she's only a dream. dream.

LET'S DO IT (LET'S FALL IN LOVE)

Words and Music by
COLE PORTER

Moderately

Verse: **Semplice** *(not fast)*

When the lit-tle blue-bird, who has nev-er said a word, starts to sing, "Spring, spring," when the lit-tle blue-bell, in the bot-tom of the dell, starts to ring: "Ding, ding," when the little blue clerk, in the middle of his work, starts a tune to the moon up above, it is nature, that's all, simply telling us to fall in love. And that's why

Refrain:
gracefully

birds do it, bees do it, even educated
sponges, they say, do it, oysters down in Oyster

E♭6 E♭m6 B♭ F7 B♭ E♭m(maj7)
fleas, do it, let's do it, let's fall in love.
Bay, do it, let's do it, let's fall in love.
B♭ F+ B♭ F7
In Spain, the best upper sets do it,
Cold Cape Cod clams, 'gainst their wish, do it,
mf
p
B♭ E♭6 E♭m6 B♭
Lith - u - a - ni - ans and Letts do it, let's do it,
e - ven la - zy jel - ly - fish do it, let's do it,
F7 B♭ E♭6 B♭ Gm
let's fall in love. The Dutch in old Am - ster -
let's fall in love. E - lec - tric eels, I might
mf

Cm7
B♭
B♭7
E♭
dam do it, not to men - tion the Finns. Folks in Si -
add, do it, though it shocks 'em, I know. Why ask if
mp
A♭7
D♭
B♭m7
F7
F+
B♭
am do it; think of Si - a - mese twins. Some Ar - gen - tines, with-out
shad do it? Wait - er, bring me shad roe. In shal - low shoals, En-glish
mf
p
F7
B♭
E♭7
means, do it, peo - ple say, in Bos - ton, e - ven beans do it,
soles do it, gold - fish, in the pri - va - cy of bowls, do it,
cresc.
B♭
Gm7
Cm7(♭5)
F7
B♭
E♭m(maj7)
1.
B♭
F+
2.
B♭
let's do it, let's fall in love. Ro - man - tic
let's do it, let's fall in love.
mf un poco allarg.
a tempo
mf
sf

Original Lyrics (complete)

Verse:
When the little bluebird,
Who has never said a word,
Starts to sing, "Spring, spring,"
When the little bluebell,
In the bottom of the dell,
Starts to ring: "Ding, ding,"
When the little blue clerk,
In the middle of his work,
Starts a tune to the moon up above,
It is nature, that's all,
Simply telling us to fall in love.

Refrain 1:
*And that's why Chinks do it, Japs do it,
Up in Lapland, little Lapps do it,
Let's do it, let's fall in love.
In Spain, the best upper sets do it,
Lithuanians and Letts do it,
Let's do it, let's fall in love.
The Dutch in old Amsterdam do it,
Not to mention the Finns.
Folks in Siam do it;
Think of Siamese twins.
Some Argentines, without means, do it,
People say, in Boston, even beans do it,
Let's do it, let's fall in love.

Refrain 2:
The nightingales, in the dark, do it,
Larks, k-razy for a lark, do it,
Let's do it, let's fall in love.
Canaries, caged in the house, do it,
When they're out of season, grouse do it,
Let's do it, let's fall in love.
The most sedate barnyard fowls do it,
When a chanticleer cries.
High-browed old owls do it,
They're supposed to be wise.
Penguins in flocks, on the rocks, do it,
Even little cuckoos, in their clocks, do it,
Let's do it, let's fall in love.

Refrain 3:
Romantic sponges, they say, do it,
Oysters down in Oyster Bay do it,
Let's do it, let's fall in love.
Cold Cape Cod clams, 'gainst their wish, do it,
Even lazy jellyfish do it,
Let's do it, let's fall in love.
Electric eels, I might add, do it,
Though it shocks 'em, I know.
Why ask if shad do it?
Waiter, bring me shad roe.
In shallow shoals, English soles do it,
Goldfish, in the privacy of bowls, do it,
Let's do it, let's fall in love.

Refrain 3: (English Production)
Young whelks and winkles, in pubs, do it,
Little sponges, in their tubs, do it,
Let's do it, let's fall in love.
Cold salmon, quite 'gainst their wish, do it,
Even lazy jellyfish do it,
Let's do it, let's fall in love.
The most select schools of cod do it,
Though it shocks 'em, I fear.
Sturgeon, thank God, do it,
Have some caviar, dear.
In shady shoals, English soles do it,
Goldfish, in the privacy of bowls, do it,
Let's do it, let's fall in love.

Refrain 4:
The dragonflies, in the reeds, do it,
Sentimental centipedes do it,
Let's do it, let's fall in love.
Mosquitos, heaven forbid, do it,
So does ev'ry katydid do it,
Let's do it, let's fall in love.
The most refined ladybugs do it,
When a gentleman calls.
Moths, in your rugs, do it.
What's the use of moth balls?
Locust, in trees, do it, bees do it,
Even overeducated fleas do it,
Let's do it, let's fall in love.

Refrain 5:
The chimpanzees, in the zoos, do it,
Some courageous kangaroos do it,
Let's do it, let's fall in love.
I'm sure giraffes, on the sly, do it,
Heavy hippopotami do it,
Let's do it, let's fall in love.
Old sloths who hang down from twigs do it,
Though the effort is great.
Sweet guinea pigs do it,
Buy a couple and wait.
The world admits bears, in pits, do it,
Even Pekineses, in the Ritz, do it,
Let's do it, let's fall in love.

* The opening lines of refrain 1 were changed to the familiar "Birds do it, bees do it," etc., when Porter realized that many would find the words "Chinks" and "Japs" offensive.

LET'S CALL THE WHOLE THING OFF

Music and Lyrics by
GEORGE GERSHWIN
and IRA GERSHWIN

Verse:

Things have come to a pret-ty pass,___ our ro-mance is grow-ing flat, for you like this and the oth-er___ while

I go for this and that. Good-ness knows what the end will be;— Oh, I
don't know where I'm at... It looks as if we two will nev-er be
one, some-thing must be done.

Refrain:
You say ee-ther and I say eye-ther, you say nee-ther and I say nye-ther;
You say laugh-ter and I say lawf-ter, you say af-ter and I say awf-ter;

G G7/F C/E Cm/E♭ G/D Em A7 D7
Ee - ther, eye - ther, nee - ther, nye - ther, let's call the whole thing off!
Laugh - ter, lawf - ter, af - ter, awf - ter, let's call the whole thing off!
mf
G Em9 Am7 D7(♭9) G Em9 Am7 D7(♭9)
You like po - ta - to and I like po - tah - to, you like to - ma - to and I like to - mah - to; Po -
You like va - nil - la and I like va - nel - la, You, sa's' - pa - ril - la and I, sa's' - pa - rel - la; Va -
G G7/F C/E Am7(♭5) G/B C D7sus G
ta - to, po - tah - to, to - ma - to, to - mah - to!
nil - la, va - nel - la, Choc'- late, straw - b'ry!
Let's call the whole thing off! But
C♯m7(♭5) F♯7 Bm7 E7(♭9) Am7 D9
oh! If we call the whole thing off, then we must part. And

C♯m7(♭5) F♯7 Bm7 E7(♭9) Am7 D9 D7
oh! If we ev - er part, then that might break my heart!
So, if
So, if
G Em9 Am7 D7(♭9) G Em9 Am7 D7(♭9)
you like pa - ja - mas and I like pa - jah - mas, I'll wear pa - ja - mas and give up pa - jah - mas.
you go for oys - ters and I go for ers - ters, I'll or - der oys - ters and can - cel the ers - ters.
G G7/F C/E Am7(♭5) G/B C G/B C6/E B7(♯5) B7 E7(♭9) E7
For we know we need each oth - er, so we bet - ter call the call - ing off off.
Am7 Bm D11 D7 G E♭7 D9(♯5) G F♯7/G G6/9
1. 2.
Let's call the whole thing off! off!
f

LET'S GO GET STONED

**Words and Music by
VALERIE SIMPSON, NICHOLAS ASHFORD
and JOSEPHINE ARMSTEAD**

Moderate gospel groove ♩. = 63 *Chorus:*

Let's go get stoned, oh, let's go get stoned. Ev-'ry-bod-y, let's go get stoned,

---

* Original recording 1/2 step higher in D♭.

Let's Go Get Stoned - 6 - 1

© 1965 (Renewed) WARNER-TAMERLANE PUBLISHING CORP. and RENLEIGH MUSIC INC.
All Rights for RENLEIGH MUSIC INC. Controlled and Administered by UNIVERSAL MUSIC-CAREERS
All Rights Reserved

A7
Dm
C/E
F
F/G
whoa,
let's go get stoned.
C
G7
Verse:
C9
(Spoken:) Now, wait a minute.
You know my ba - by,
F7
C9
she won't let me in.
I've got a few pen-nies,
F7
I'm gon - na buy my - self a bot - tle of gin.

148

| C | E7 | Am | F | F#dim7 |

And then I'm gon-na call my bud-dy___ on the tel-e-phone___ and say:___

| F/G | | C | G7 |

let's go get___ stoned.___ *Now, listen...*

| C9 | | F7 | |

You know I work so hard all___ day long.

| C9 | | F7 | |

Ev-'ry-thing I try to do___ seems to al-ways turn out wrong.___

Let's Go Get Stoned - 6 - 3

C
E7
Am
F
F♯dim7
That's why I wan-na stop by
on my way home and say:
F/G
C
C9
let's go get stoned. Now let me tell you one more thing...
F7
Am
Ain't no harm
to have a lit-tle taste,
F7
C9
but don't lose your cool
and start mess-ing up the man's place.

150

Ain't no harm to take a little nip, but don't you fall down and bust your lip, hmm,

Chorus:
no, no. Let's go get stoned, oh, let's go get stoned. I think ev-'ry-bod-y ought to come on and

Let's Go Get Stoned - 6 - 5

[C] go with me. Let's [E7] go get stoned, [A7] [Dm] oh, [C/E]

[F] [F/G] let's go get stoned. [C] I'm gonna tell you one more time what I'm gonna do: [G7]

[C] Let's go get stoned, [E7] [A7] [Dm] oh, [C/E]

[F] [F/G] let's go get stoned. [C] [G7]

MACK THE KNIFE

English Words by
MARC BLITZSTEIN
Original German Words by
BERT BRECHT

Music by
KURT WEILL

Moderate swing ♩ = 84

1. Oh,— the

Verses 1 & 2:

shark, babe,— has— such teeth, dear, and he shows them—
shark bites— with— its teeth, babe, scar-let bil-lows—

pearl-y whites.— Just a jack-knife
start to spread. Fan-cy gloves, though,

© 1928 (Renewed) UNIVERSAL EDITION
© 1955 (Renewed) WEILL-BRECHT-HARMS CO., INC.
Renewal Rights Assigned to the KURT WEILL FOUNDATION FOR MUSIC, BERT BRECHT and THE ESTATE OF MARC BLITZSTEIN
All Rights Administered by WB MUSIC CORP.
All Rights Reserved

Verse 3:

has old Mac-heath, babe, and he keeps it out of sight.
has old Mac-heath, babe, so there's nev-er, nev-er a trace of red.

2. You know when that
3. Now, on the side-walk, uh-huh, huh, ooh, Sun-day morn-ing, uh-huh, lies a bod-y just ooz-ing life. And some-one's

sneak-ing _____ 'round the cor - ner. _____ Could that some-

one _____ be Mack the Knife? _____ 4. There's a

Verse 4:

tug-boat down by the riv - er, don't you know, where a ce-

ment bag's just a-droop-in' on down. _____ Oh, that ce-

C/E
E♭dim7
Dm7
ment is just,_ it's there_ for the weight, dear._ Five - 'll get you
Dm7/G
C6
A♭7
ten, Old_ Mack - ie's back in town._ 5. Now, d'ja hear 'bout Lou - ie
Verse 5:
D♭6
E♭m7
Mil - ler?_ He_ dis - ap - peared,_ babe,_ af - ter
A♭7
D♭6
draw - ing out_ all_ his hard-earned cash. And now Mac-heath_

D♭/F
Edim7
E♭m7
A♭
E♭m7
A♭
spends just like a sail - or. Could it be
E♭m7
A♭7
D♭6
A7
our boy's done some-thing rash? 6. Now, Jen-ny Div -
Verse 6:
D6
Em7
er, yeah, Su-key Taw - dry, ooh, Miss
A7
D6
Lot-te Len-ya, and old Lu-cy Brown. Ooh, the

line forms on the right, babe, now that Mack-ie's back in town. 7. I said, Jen-ny Div-

Verse 7:

er, Su-key Taw-dry, look out to Miss Lot-te Len-ya, and old Lu-cy Brown. Yes, that *line forms on the right, babe, now that Mack-ie's back in town.*

Look out, old Mack-ie is back!

Mack the Knife - 7 - 7

MAKIN' WHOOPEE!

Words by GUS KAHN
Music by WALTER DONALDSON

An-oth-er bride, an-oth-er June, an-oth-er sun-ny hon-ey-moon, an-oth-er sea-son, an-oth-er year or may-be less. What's this I hear? Well, can't you guess? She feels neg-lect-ed and he's sus-

rea - son___ for mak-in' whoop-ee! A lot of shoes,___ a lot of
pect - ed___ of mak-in' whoop-ee! She sits a - lone___ most ev-'ry

rice.___ The groom is ner - vous,___ he an-swers twice.___ It's real - ly
night.___ He does-n't phone her,___ he does-n't write.___ He says's he's

kill - ing___ that he's so will - ing___ to make whoop-ee.___
"bus - y",___ but she says "Is he?"___ He's mak-in' whoop-ee.___

Pic - ture a lit - tle love nest down where the ros - es cling.
He does-n't make much mon - ey, on - ly five thou-sand per.

G♯dim7 Am Cm6 G
Pic - ture the same sweet love nest, think what a year can bring. He's wash - ing
Some judge who thinks he's fun - ny says, "You'll pay six to her." He says, "Now
D7 G7
dish - es and ba - by clothes. He's so am - bi - tious he ev - en
judge, sup - pose I fail?" The judge says, "Budge right in - to
C Cm G E♭7 D7
sews. But don't for - get folks, that's what you get folks for mak - in'
jail. You'd bet - ter keep her. I think it's cheap - er than mak - in'
1. 2.
G Am7(♭5) D7 G C7 G
whoop - ee! An - oth - er whoop - ee!"
f

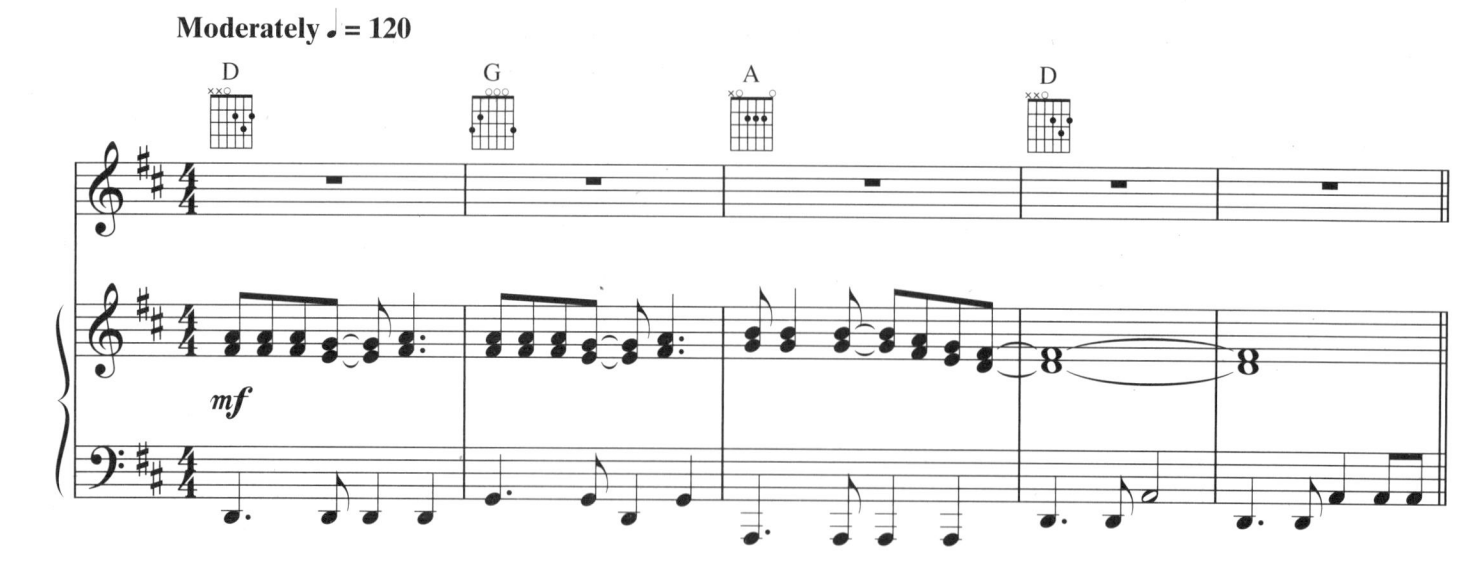

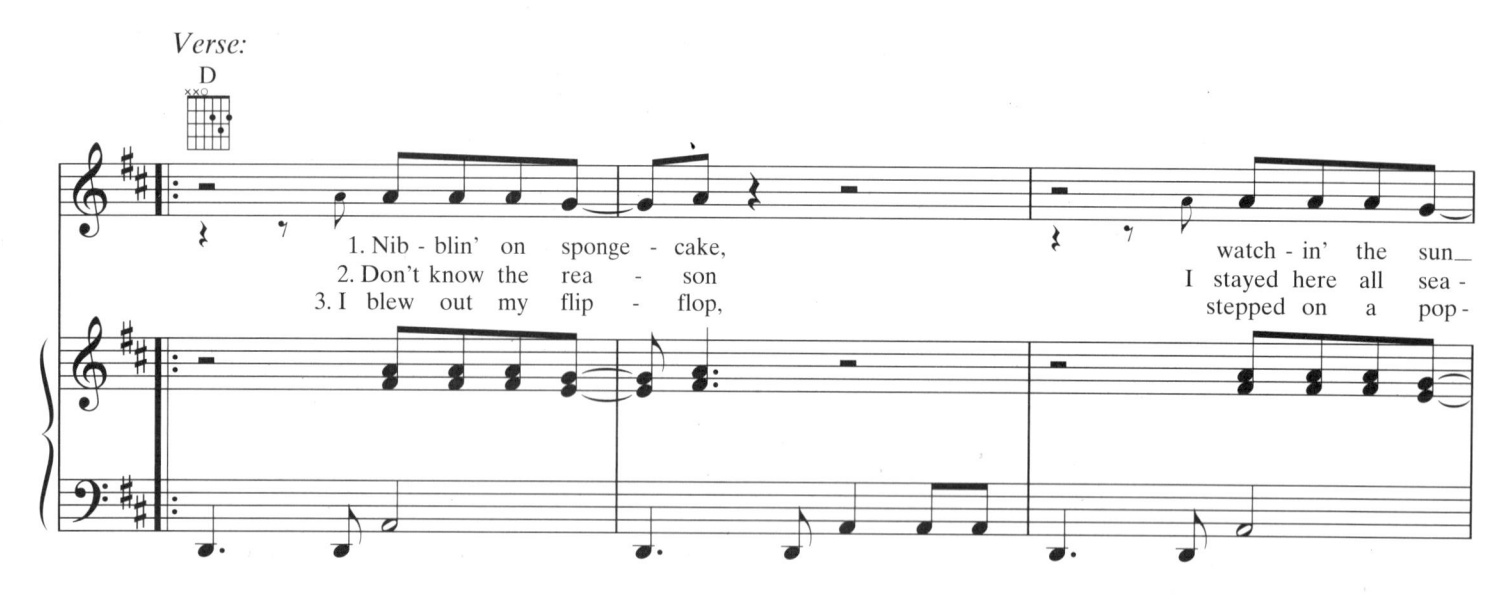

MARGARITAVILLE

Words and Music by
JIMMY BUFFETT

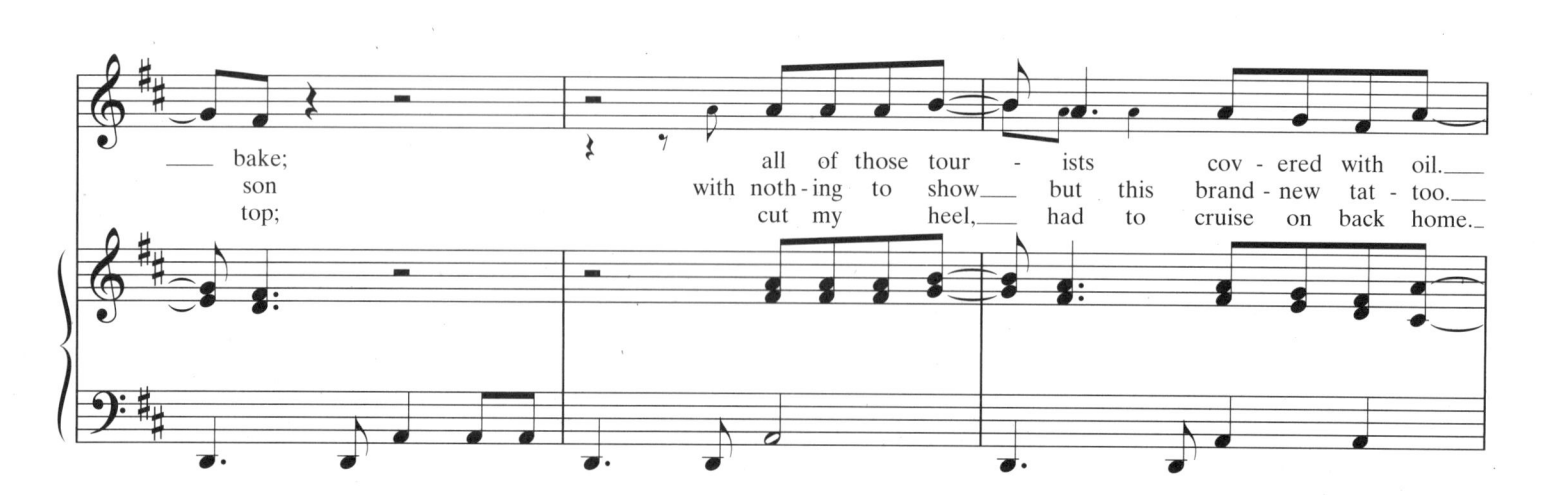

Moderately ♩ = 120

Verse:

1. Nib-blin' on sponge-cake, watch-in' the sun bake; all of those tour-ists cov-ered with oil.
2. Don't know the rea-son I stayed here all sea-son with noth-ing to show but this brand-new tat-too.
3. I blew out my flip-flop, stepped on a pop-top; cut my heel, had to cruise on back home.

© 1977 (Renewed) CORAL REEFER MUSIC
All Rights Reserved

Strum-min' my six - string on my front porch swing.
But it's a real beau - ty, a Mex-i-can cu - tie, Smell those shrimp; how it got they're be-gin-ning to boil.
But there's booze in the blend-er, and soon it will ren-der that fro-zen con- here I have-n't a clue.
coc-tion that helps me hang on.

Chorus:
Wast-in' a-way a-gain in Mar-ga-ri-ta-ville,

G
A
D
search - in' for my lost shak - er of salt.
D7
G
A
Some people claim that there's a
D
A/C#
G
A
wom - an to blame,
but I know
now I think,
but I know
1.2.
D
it's no - bod - y's fault.
hell, it could be my fault.
it's my own damn fault.

3.
D
G
Yes, and some_ peo - ple claim_
A
D
A/C♯
G
_ that there's_ a wom - an to blame,_ and I know_
A
D
it's my own_ damn_ fault._
G
A
D

MISTY

Words by
JOHNNY BURKE

Music by
ERROLL GARNER

Slowly, with expression

© 1954, 1955 (Copyrights Renewed) MARKE-MUSIC PUBLISHING CO., INC., LIMERICK MUSIC CORPORATION,
MY DAD'S SONGS, INC., REGANESQUE MUSIC and OCTAVE MUSIC PUBLISHING CORP.
All Rights for MARKE-MUSIC PUBLISHING CO., INC. Administered by WB MUSIC CORP.
All Rights Reserved

B♭m9 E♭7(♭9) A♭maj7 A♭m9 D♭13
thou-sand vi-o-lins be-gin to play, or it might be the sound of your hel-lo, that
E♭maj9 Cm Fm7 B♭7(♭9) E♭ Cm7 Fm7 B♭7(♭9)
mu - sic I hear. I get mist - y the mo-ment you're near.
E♭6 Ddim7 E♭6 B♭m7 E♭7 E♭7(♭9)
You can say that you're lead-ing me on, but it's just what I
A♭maj9 A♭6 B♭dim7 A♭6 Am7(4)
want you to do. Don't you no-tice how hope-less-ly I'm lost?

That's why I'm fol-low-ing you. On my own, would I wan-der through this won-der-land a-lone, nev-er know-ing my right foot from my left, my hat from my glove? I'm too mist-y and too much in love.

Look at love.

MOONDANCE

Words and Music by
VAN MORRISON

Jazz shuffle ♩ = 132

Verse:

(3.) mar - vel - ous night__ for a moon - dance with__ the stars up a - bove in your eyes,
(2.) wan - na make love__ to you to - night, I____ can't wait 'til the morn - ing has come.

a fan - ta - bu - lous night__ to make ro - mance 'neath the
And I know now the time____ is just__ right and straight

© 1970 (Renewed) WB MUSIC CORP. and CALEDONIA SOUL MUSIC
All Rights Administered by WB MUSIC CORP.
All Rights Reserved

Am7 Bm7 Am7 Bm7 Am7 Bm7 Am7 Bm7
cov-er of Oc - to-ber skies. And all the leaves on the trees are fall-ing to the
in-to my arms_ you will run. And when you come, my heart will be wait-ing to make
Am7 Bm7 Am7 Bm7 Am7 Bm7
sound of the breez-es that blow. And I'm try-ing to please_ to the call -
sure that you're nev-er a-lone. There and then, all my dreams_ will come true,_
Am7 Bm7 Am7 Bm7 Am7
ing of your heart-strings that play soft and low. And all the
_ dear, there and then, will I make you my own. And ev-'ry
Dm6 Am7 Dm6 Am7
night's_ mag - ic seems to whis - per and hush, and all the
time I_ touch_ you, you just trem - ble in-side. And I know

Dm6
Am7
N.C.
Dm6
N.C.
E7(♯5)
Am7
soft moon - light seems to shine in your blush.
how much you want me; that, you can't hide.
Can I
Chorus:
Dm7
Am7
just have one more moon - dance with you, my love?
Can I just make some more ro - mance with you,
To Coda
1.
E7
2.
E7
my love?
2. Well, I

Piano solo:
Am7 Bm7 Am7 Bm7 Am7 Bm7
(play straight 8th notes)
8va
Am7 Bm7 Am7 Bm7 Am7 Bm7
(8va)
Am7 Bm7 Am7 Bm7 Am7 Bm7
Am7 Bm7 Am7 Bm7 Am7 Bm7

Saxophone solo:

Dm7
Am7
Dm7
Am7
Dm7
Am7
Dm7
Am7
Dm7
Am7
Dm7
Am7
D.S. 𝄋 al Coda
𝄌 Coda
Dm7
Am7
E7
E7
3. Well, it's a
One more moon -
Am7
Bm7
Am7
Bm7
Am7
Bm7
Am7
Bm7
dance with you in the moon-light, on a

175

mag-ic night. La la la la, in the moon-light, on a mag-ic night. Can't I just have one more moon-dance with you, my love?

Moondance - 7 - 7

THEME FROM "NEW YORK, NEW YORK"

Words by
FRED EBB

Music by
JOHN KANDER

Moderately, with rhythm

Start spreadin' the news, I'm leav-ing to-day, I want to be a part__ of it; New York, New York. These vag-a-bond

Theme From "New York, New York" - 5 - 1

© 1977 (Renewed) UNITED ARTISTS CORPORATION
All Rights Controlled by EMI Unart Catalog Inc. (Publishing) and ALFRED MUSIC PUBLISHING CO., INC. (Print)
All Rights Reserved

shoes are long-ing to stray   right through the very heart of it; New York, New York.   I____ want to

Bridge 1:
wake up   in a cit-y that does-n't sleep   and find I'm king of the hill,___   top of the heap.   These lit-tle town

Verse 2:

D
Em7
A7
Em7
A7
blues are melt-ing a - way, I'll make a
D
A/C♯
Bm7
B♭m7
Am9
D7
brand-new start_ of it in old New York.___ If I can
Gmaj7
Gm6
D/A
B7(♭9)
Em7
F♯m7
make it there,___ I'll make it an - y - where.___ It's up to you, New
Gmaj7
A9
D
Em7
B♭7
F7
B♭7
York, New York.

E♭
E♭maj7
E♭7
B♭m7 E♭7
New York, New York. I want to
Bridge 2:
A♭
A♭m6
E♭maj7
Fm7 F♯m7
wake up in a cit-y that nev-er sleeps and find I'm
mf
Gm7
C7
C♭maj7
B♭7
"A" Num-ber One, top of the list, king of the hill, "A" Num-ber One.
rit.
Freely
Slower ♩ = 80
B♭11
N.C.
E♭maj7
Fm7
B♭7
E♭maj7
These lit-tle town blues are melt-ing a-way,
f

Theme From "New York, New York"

NIGHT AND DAY

Words and Music by
COLE PORTER

Verse:

Like the beat, beat, beat of the tom-tom, when the jungle shadows fall, like the tick, tick, tock of the stately clock, as it stands against the wall, like the

A♭7 D♭ A7 D/F♯ Fdim7
drip, drip, drip of the rain - drops, when the sum - mer show'r is through, so a
C/E Cm/E♭ G/D C♯dim7 C G/B Gm/B♭ Am7
voice with - in me keeps re - peat - ing, you, you, you. Night and day
Refrain:
A♭maj7 G7 G+ Cmaj7 C6
you are the one, on - ly you
p – mf
A♭maj7 G7 G+ Cmaj7 C6
be - neath the moon and un - der the sun. Wheth - er

near to me or far, it's no matter, darling, where you are, I think of you night and day.

Day and night, why is it so, that this long-

A♭maj7 G7 G+ Cmaj7 C6
ing for you fol - lows wher - ev - er I go? In the
F♯m7(♭5) Fm7 Em7 E♭dim7
roar - ing traf - fic's boom, in the si - lence of my lone - ly room, I
r.h.
Dm7 G7 C
think of you night and day. Night and
E♭ C
day, un - der the hide of me there's an
mf espr.

oh, such a hungry yearning burning inside of me. And its tor-ment won't be through 'til you let me spend my life making love to you day and night, night and day.

Night and day

ORANGE COLORED SKY

Words and Music by
MILTON DELUGG and
WILLIE STEIN

Walking tempo

Chorus: (Wistfully)

I was walk-in' a-long mind-in' my bus-'ness when out of an or-ange col-ored sky,

Violent

Flash! Bam!

(crash) (crash)

Violent

Orange Colored Sky - 4 - 1

© 1950 (Renewed) AMY DEE MUSIC CORP.
All Rights Reserved

B♭ G7 Cm7 F7 B♭ Bdim7 F7
A - la - ka - zam! Won - der - ful you came by. I was
mp–mf
B♭6 Bdim7 Cm7 C♯dim7 B♭ A♭maj7
hum - min' a tune, drink - in' in sun - shine when out of that or - ange col - ored
Violent
G9 Cm7 C♯dim7 B♭ G7
view, Flash! Bam! A - la - ka - zam!
(crash) (crash)
Cm7 F7 B♭6 Cm7 B♭ B♭7(♯5) E♭
I got a look at you. One look and I yelled
mp–mf

"Tim - ber! Watch out for fly - ing glass!" 'Cause the ceil - ing fell in, and the bot - tom fell out, I went in - to a spin, and I start - ed to shout, "I've been hit! This is it! This is it!" I was walk - in' a - long mind - in' my bus - 'ness when love came and hit me in the eye.

Violent
Cm7 C♯dim7 B♭ G7 Cm7 F7(♭9)
Flash! Bam! A - la - ka - zam! Out of an or - ange col - ored
(crash) (crash)
B♭ Cm7 B♭ F7 Cm7 B7
sky. I was or - ange col - ored, pur - ple striped,
E♭6 E♭m6 B♭ D7(♭5) G7 Cm7
pret - ty green, pol - ka - dot - ted sky. Flash! Bam!
(crash) (crash)
F7 B♭ A♭13(♯11) B♭6/9
A - la - ka - zam! and good - bye.

THE PINK PANTHER

By HENRY MANCINI

Bridge:
Swing

Gm
E♭9
D9
Gm6
Solo:
Em6
(Inst. solo ad lib.…
C13
Em6
F13
Em6
C13
Em6
C7
B7
Em
Tempo I
…end solo)
mp
mf

Verse:

RAINDROPS KEEP FALLIN' ON MY HEAD

Words by
HAL DAVID

Music by
BURT BACHARACH

Moderately slow ♩ = 104

Verse 1:

1. Rain-drops keep fall-in' on my head, and just like the guy whose feet are too big for his bed, noth-in' seems to fit. Those rain-drops are fall-in' on my head, they keep fall-in'. 2. So I just

Raindrops Keep Fallin' on My Head - 4 - 1

© 1969 (Renewed) NEW HIDDEN VALLEY MUSIC, CASA DAVID and WB MUSIC CORP.
All Rights on behalf of itself and NEW HIDDEN VALLEY MUSIC Administered by WB MUSIC CORP.
All Rights Reserved

Verse 2:

did me some talkin' to the sun, and I said I didn't like the way he got things done, sleepin' on the job. Those raindrops are fallin' on my head, they keep fallin'. But there's one

Bridge:

thing I know: The blues they send to meet
me. *Instrumental...*

me won't de-feat me. *...end Instrumental*

It won't be long till hap-pi-ness steps up to greet me.

Verse 3:

3. Rain-drops keep fall-in' on my head, but that does-n't mean my eyes will soon be turn-in' red, cry-in's not for

Am7
D7
Gm7
me 'cause I'm nev - er gon - na stop the rain by com - plain - in',
B♭/C
C
F
Fmaj7
1.
Gm7
B♭/C
be - cause I'm free.
Noth - in's wor - ry - in'
2.
Gm7
B♭/C
N.C.
Noth - in's wor - ry - in' me.
Fast latin beat ♩ = 180 (♫ = ♩♪)
Repeat ad lib. and fade
Fmaj7
E♭maj7

SATIN DOLL

Words and Music by
JOHNNY MERCER, DUKE ELLINGTON
and BILLY STRAYHORN

© 1958 (Renewed) WB MUSIC CORP., SONY/ATV HARMONY and TEMPO MUSIC INC.
All Rights Reserved

Dm7 G7 Em7 A7 Em7 A7
out skip - pin'? Care - ful, a - mi - go, you're flip - pin'.
Cm/E♭ D7 A♭m7 D♭7(♭9) C6 D9 G7(♭9) C6
Speaks Lat - in, that Sat - in Doll. She's
Gm7 C7 Gm7 C7 F
no - bod - y's fool, so I'm play - ing it cool as can be.
Am7 D7 Am7 D7
I'll give it a whirl, but I ain't for no girl catch - ing me.

Satin Doll - 3 - 3

THIS MASQUERADE

Words and Music by
LEON RUSSELL

Fm7
Fm(maj7)
Fm7
Are we real-ly hap - py here with this lone - ly game we play,
Bb13
Fm9
Db7
look-ing for words to say?
Gm11
C7(b9 #5)
Fm7
Search-ing but not find-
Fm(maj7)
Fm7
Bb9
ing un - der - stand - ing an - y - way, we're

D♭13(♯11)
C7
Fm7
lost in a mas, mas - quer-ade.
Em7
A13
E♭m9
A♭13(♭9)
Both a - fraid to say we're just too far
D♭maj9
B♭7(♭9 ♯5)
E♭m9
a - way from be - ing close to - geth-
A♭13(♭9)
D♭maj7
er from the start. We

tried to talk it o-ver, but the words got in the way.

We're lost in-side this lone-ly game we play. Thoughts of leav-ing dis-

ap-pear ev-'ry time I see your eyes,

Fm7
D♭9
Gm11
no mat-ter how hard I try
C7(♯9 ♯5)
Fm7
Fm(maj7)
to un-der-stand the rea - sons that we
Fm7
B♭9
D♭13
C7(♯9 ♯5)
car-ry on this way. We're lost in a mas - quer-ade.
Repeat ad lib. and fade
Fm7
B♭13
Fm7
B♭13

SAVE THE LAST DANCE FOR ME

Words by DOC POMUS
Music by MORT SHUMAN

Moderately

Verse:

1. You can dance ev-'ry dance with the guy who gave you the eye; let him hold you tight. You can
   know that the mu-sic is fine, like spar-kling wine; go and have your fun. Laugh and

smile, ev-'ry smile for the man who held your hand 'neath the
sing, but while we're a-part, don't give your heart to

© 1960 (Renewed) by UNICHAPPELL MUSIC INC.
All Rights Reserved

pale moon-light. / *an-y-one.* But don't for-get who's tak-ing you home and in whose arms you're gon-na be. So, dar-lin', save the last dance for me.

2. Oh, I me.

Bridge: Ba-by, don't you know I love you so?

E♭
N.C.
Can't you feel it when we touch?
I will nev - er, nev - er
B♭7
E♭
let you go.
I love you, oh, so much.
Verse:
You can dance, go and car - ry on till the
B♭7
night is gone and it's time to go.
If he

asks if you're all a-lone,__ can he take you home,__ you must tell him no.__ 'Cause don't for-get who's tak-ing you home and in whose arms you're gon-na be.__ So, dar-lin',____ save the last dance for me.

THE SHADOW OF YOUR SMILE

Lyric by
PAUL FRANCIS WEBSTER

Music by
JOHNNY MANDEL

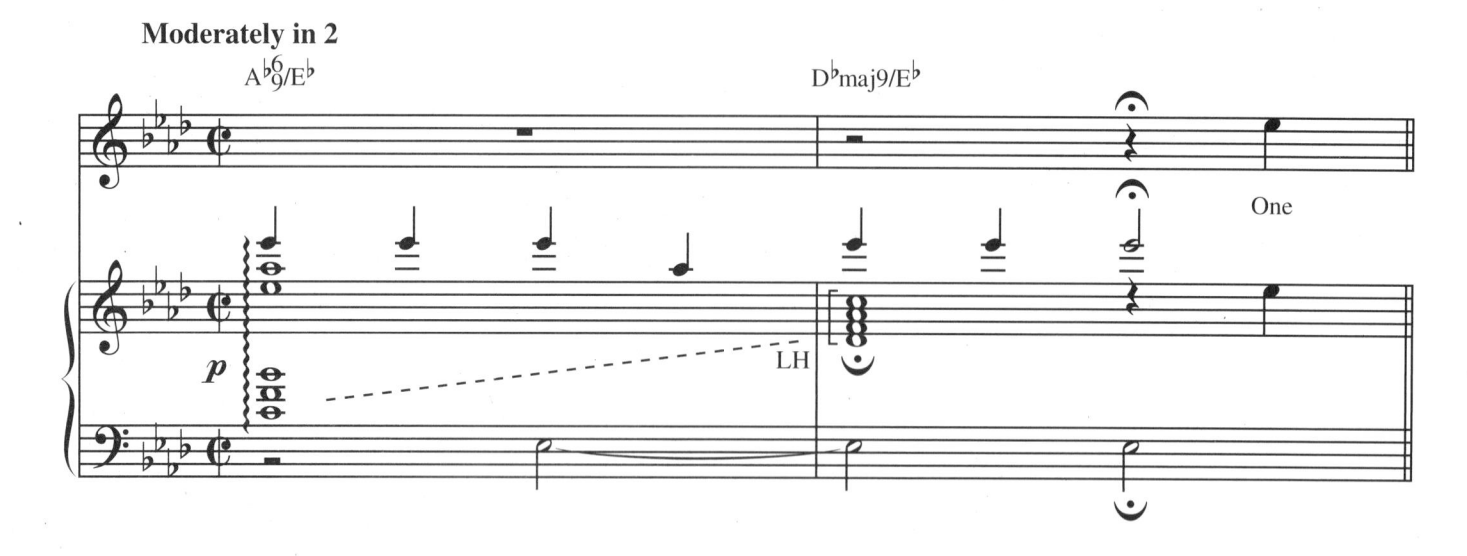

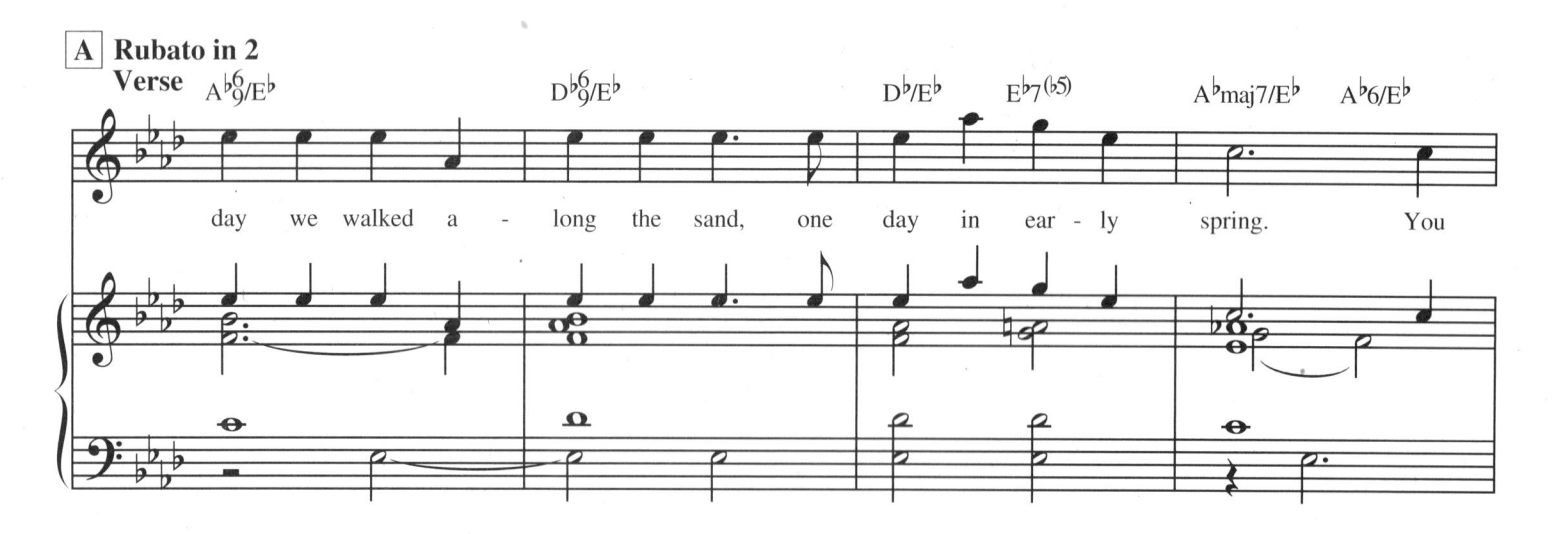

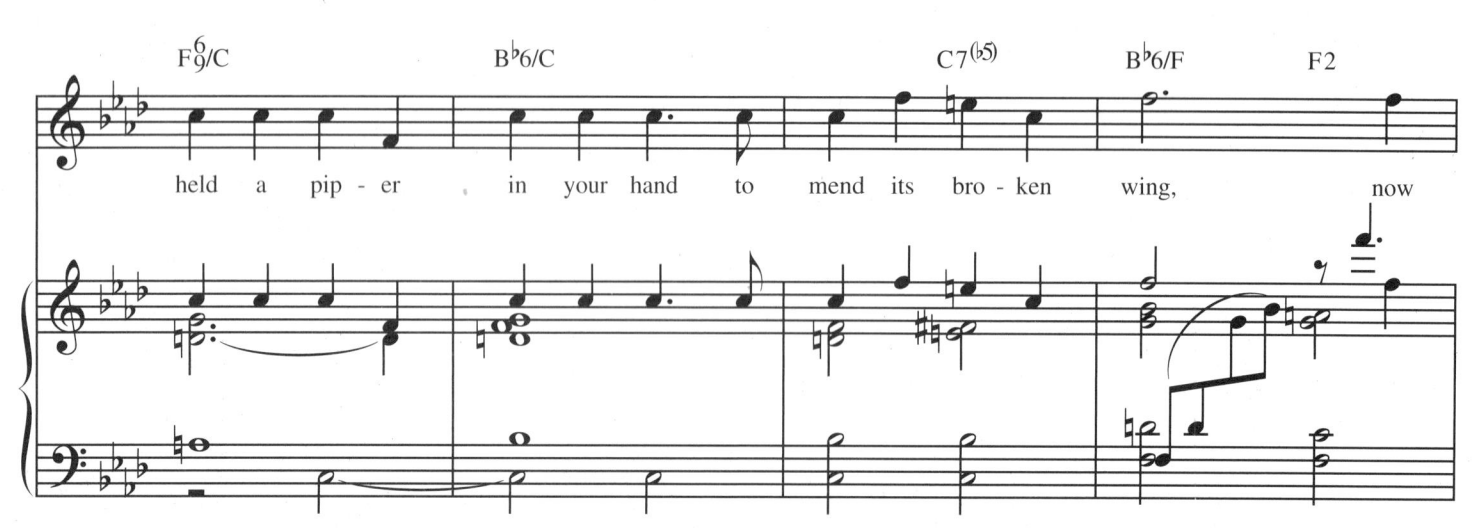

Moderately in 2

A **Rubato in 2**
Verse

One day we walked a-long the sand, one day in ear-ly spring. You held a pip-er in your hand to mend its bro-ken wing, now

The Shadow of Your Smile - 4 - 1

© 1965 METRO-GOLDWYN-MAYER INC.
Copyright Renewed by EMI Miller Catalog Inc. and Marissa Music
All Rights Controlled by EMI Miller Catalog Inc. (Publishing) and ALFRED MUSIC PUBLISHING CO., INC. (Print)
All Rights Reserved

E♭m7 F7(♭9) B♭m B♭m7/A♭ Gm7(♭5) C7(♭9 +5) Fm9 Fm F♯m9
I'll re - mem - ber man - y a day and man - y a lone - ly mile. The
Fm9 B♭13(♭5) (noB♭) Gm7 Cm9 Fm7 B♭sus4 B♭7 A♭6/E♭ E♭6/9(maj7)
ech - o of a pip - er's song, The Shad - ow of Your Smile.
LH
A Tempo - Moderate Slow 4 ♩ = 80
Chorus
Slow Rubato
B
Dm9 Dm7 G13 G7(♭9 +5) Cm7
The Shad - ow of Your Smile when you are gone
Ped.
F13 Fm9 Fm7 B♭13 B♭7(♭9 +5) E♭6/9
will col - or all my dreams and light the dawn.

A♭maj9(6) Dm7(♭5) A♭13 Fmaj9/G G7(♭9/+5) Cm Cm9 Cm
Look in - to my eyes my love and see
Cm9/B♭ Cm/B♭ Am7(♭5) D13(♭9) D7(♭9/+5) Dm7/G
all the love-ly things you are to me.
G13 C Dm9 Dm7 G13 G7(♭9/+5) Cm7
Our wist-ful lit - tle star was far too high.
F13 Fm9 Fm7 B♭13 B♭13(♭9)/A♭ B♭7(♭9/+5)/A♭
A tear - drop kissed your lips and so did
RH
Ped.

Gm7(♭5) G♭9/C Fm7 Fm6 Fm7
I. Now when I re - mem - ber spring,
A♭m7/D♭ D♭13 Gm7 D♭13(♭5) C13 C7(♭9 +5) F9 B13(♭5)
all the joy that love can bring, I will be re - mem - ber - ing
A♭6/B♭ A♭m9/B♭ B♭7(♭9 +5)
1. E♭6 9
The Shad - ow of Your Smile The Shad - ow of Your
2. C♭maj7 F♭maj7 E♭6 9
Smile.
8va
8va

THEME FROM "A SUMMER PLACE"

Words by
MACK DISCANT

Music by
MAX STEINER

Slowly, in 2 ♩. = 63

F
Dm7
Gm7
C9
F
Dm7
Gm7
C9
F
Dm7
Gm7
C9
F
Dm7
Gm7
C9
Bridge:
Dm7
B♭
Gm7
F/A
Dm7
Gm7
B♭m6
F/C
G9
B♭/C
C7
Verse:
F
Dm7
Gm7
C9
F
Dm7
Gm7
C9

F
Dm7
Gm7
C9
F
Dm7
Gm7
C9
F
Dm7
Gm7
C9
F
Dm7
Gm7
C9
F
cresc.
D
Bm7
Em7
A9
D
Bm7
Em7
A9
mf
D
Bm7
Em7
A9
D
Bm7
Em7
A9

D Bm7 Em7 A9 D Bm7 Em7 A9
D Bm7 Em7 A9 D Bm7 Em7 A9
D Bm7 Em7 A9 D Bm7 Em7 A9
Repeat ad lib. and fade
D Bm7 Em7 A9 D Bm7 Em7 A9

SUMMER WIND

English Words by JOHNNY MERCER
Original German Lyrics by HANS BRADTKE

Music by HENRY MAYER

Summer Wind

and the sum-mer wind. 2. Like

Verse 2:

paint-ed kites, those days and nights, they went fly-ing by. The world was new be-neath a blue um-brel-la sky. Then *soft-er than that pip-er man, one day it called to you. I lost you, I lost you to the sum-mer wind.*

Verse 3:
3. The au-tumn wind and the win-ter winds, they have come and gone.

222

And still the days, those lone-ly days, they go on and on. And guess who sighs his lul-la-bies through nights that nev-er end? My fick-le friend, the

F6/9
D7(♯9)
Gm9
G♭maj7(♯11)
sum-mer wind,
the
F6/9
sum-mer wind,
warm
sum-mer wind,
mm,
sum - mer wind.

TAKE FIVE

By PAUL DESMOND

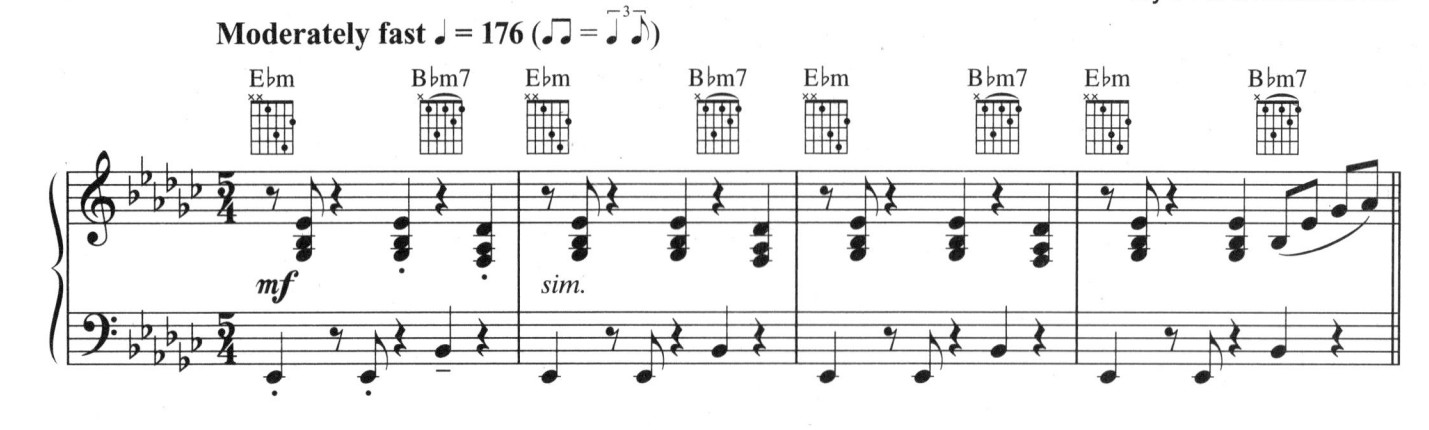

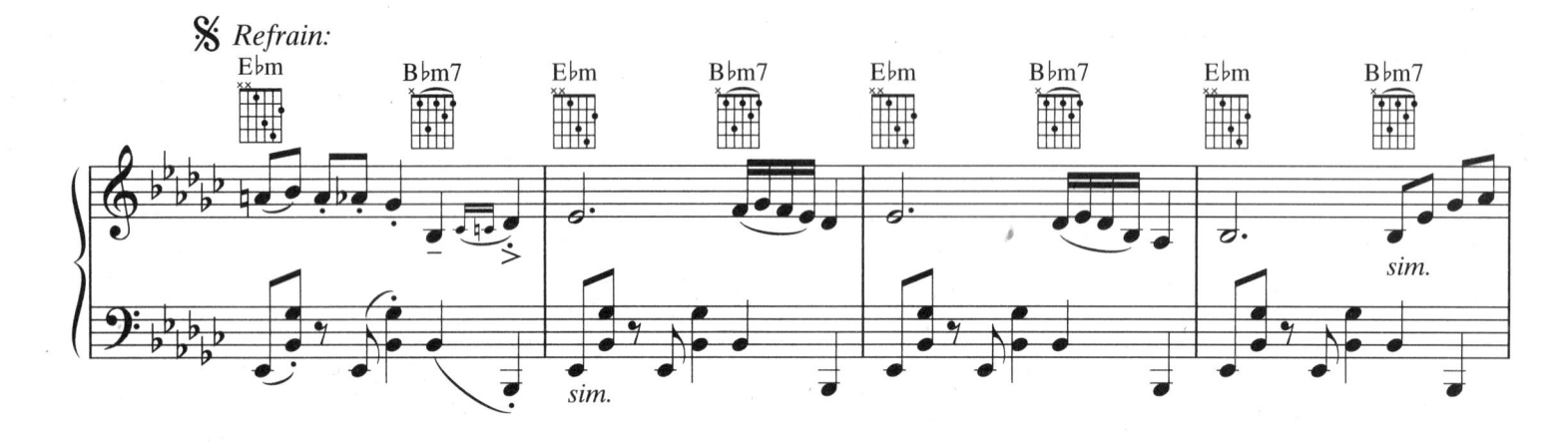

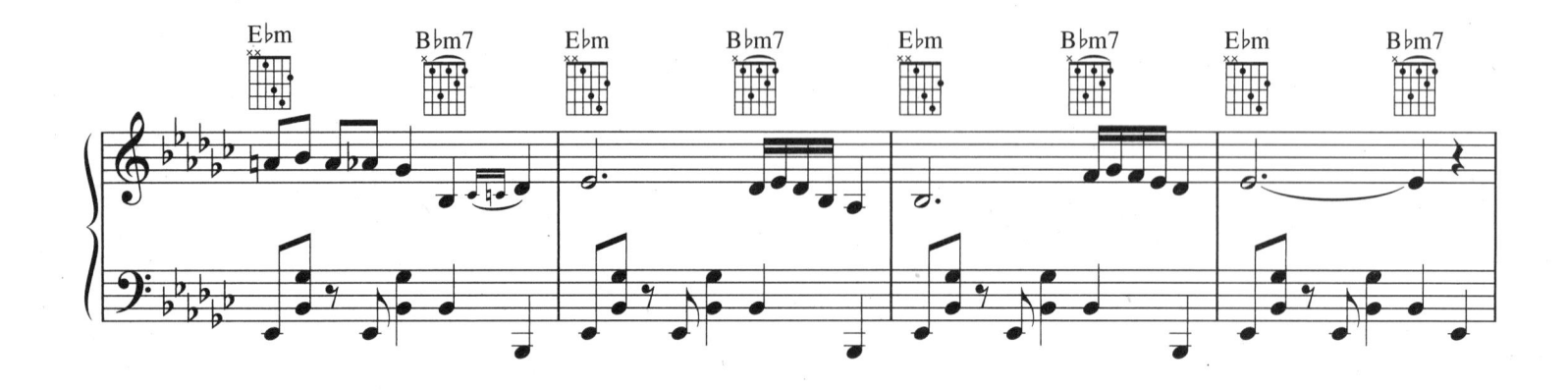

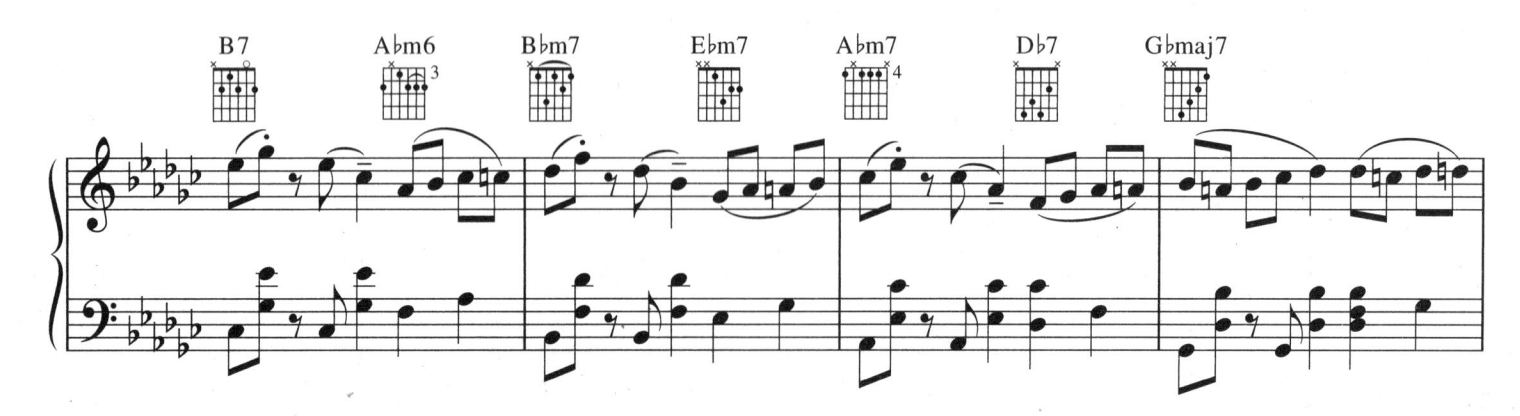

Moderately fast ♩ = 176

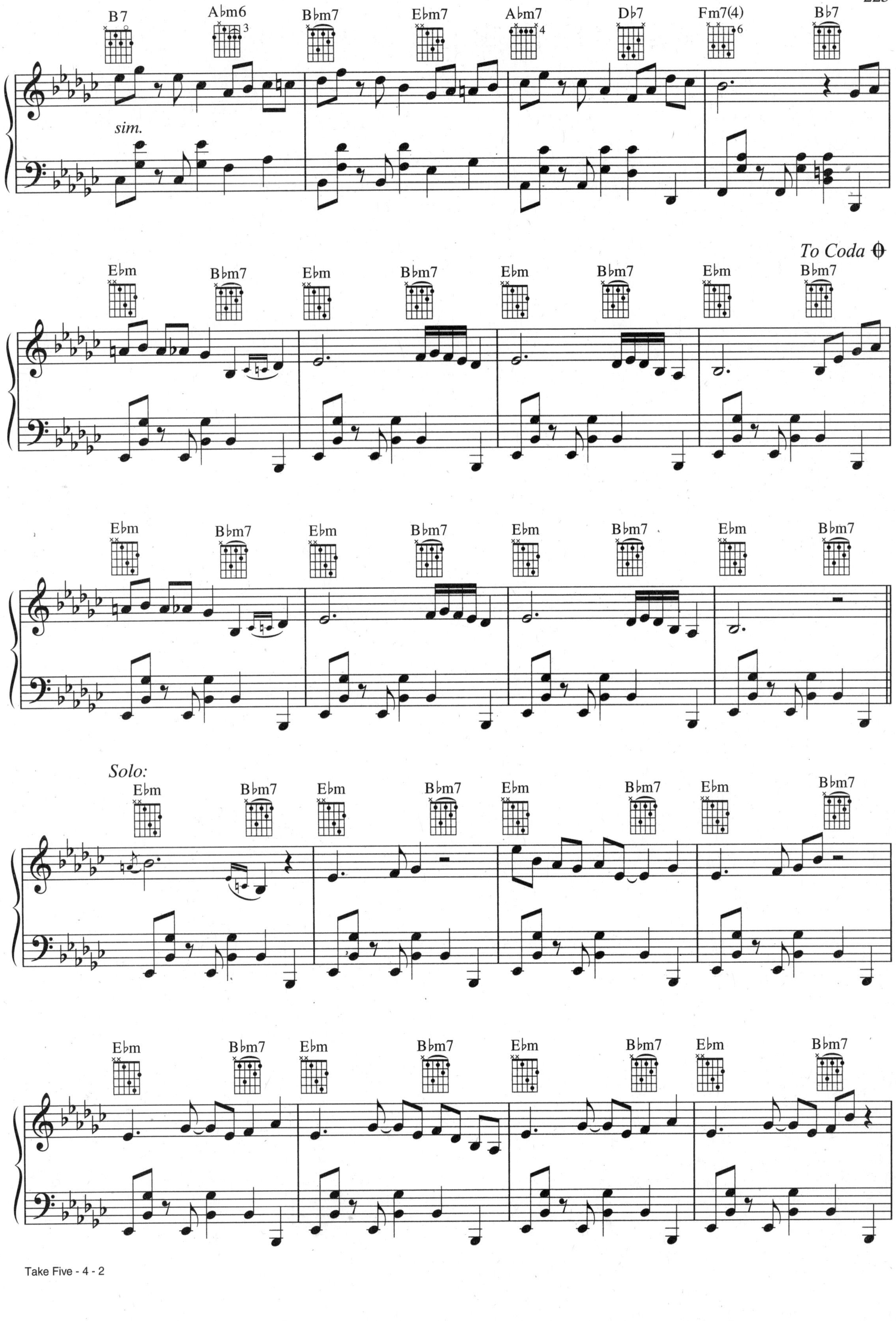
B7
A♭m6
B♭m7
E♭m7
A♭m7
D♭7
Fm7(4)
B♭7
sim.
To Coda
E♭m
B♭m7
Solo:

Ebm Bbm7 Ebm Bbm7 Ebm Bbm7 Ebm Bbm7
Ebm Bbm7 Ebm Bbm7 Ebm Bbm7 Ebm Bbm7
Ebm Bbm7 Ebm Bbm7 Ebm Bbm7 Ebm Bbm7
Ebm Bbm7 Ebm Bbm7 Ebm Bbm7 Ebm Bbm7
Ebm Bbm7 Ebm Bbm7 Ebm Bbm7
mf

D.S. 𝄋 al Coda
Ebm
Bbm7
Ebm
Bbm7
Ebm
Bbm7
sim.
Coda
Ebm
Bbm7
Ebm
Bbm7
Ebm
Bbm7
Ebm
Bbm7
Ebm
Bbm7
Ebm
Bbm7
Ebm
Bbm7
Ebm
Bbm7
Ebm
Bbm7
Ebm
Bbm7
Ebm
Bbm7
Ebm
Bbm7
Ebm
dim.
p

Taking a Chance on Love

Words by
JOHN LATOUCHE
and TED FETTER

Music by
VERNON DUKE

Verse: thought love's game was o-ver; La-dy Luck had gone a-way. I laid my cards on the ta-ble, un-a-ble to play. Then I heard good for-tune say,_____ "They're deal-ing you a new hand to-day!" Oh...

Chorus:

1. Here I go a-gain;___ I hear those trum-pets blow a-gain.___
2. Here I come a-gain;___ I'm gon-na make things hum a-gain.___
3. Here I slip a-gain,___ a-bout to take that tip a-gain.___

All a-glow a-gain,___ tak-ing a chance on love.
Act-ing dumb a-gain,___ tak-ing a chance on love.
Got my grip a-gain,___ tak-ing a chance on love.

Here I slide a-gain,___ a-bout to take that ride a-gain,___
Here I stand a-gain,___ a-bout to beat the band a-gain,___
Now I prove a-gain___ that I can make life move a-gain;___

star - ry - eyed a-gain,___ tak-ing a chance on love. I
feel - ing grand a-gain,___ tak-ing a chance on love. I
in the groove a-gain,___ tak-ing a chance on love. I

thought that cards___ were a frame - up___ I nev - er___ would try. But
nev - er dreamed___ in my slum - bers___ and bets were___ ta - boo. But
walk a - round___ with a horse - shoe; in clo - ver___ I lie. And

Taking a Chance on Love - 4 - 3

now I'm tak - ing the game up__ and the ace of hearts is high.
now I'm play - ing the num - bers__ on a lit - tle dream for two.
broth - er rab - bit, of course, you__ bet - ter kiss your foot good - bye.

Things are mend - ing now;__ I see a rain - bow blend - ing now.__ We'll have our hap - py
Wad - ing in a - gain;__ I'm lead - ing with my chin a - gain.__ I'm start - in' out to
On the ball a - gain;__ I'm rid - ing for a fall a - gain.__ I'm gon - na give my

end - ing now,__ tak - ing a chance on love. love.__
win a - gain,__ tak - ing a chance on love.
all a - gain,__ tak - ing a chance on

Taking a Chance on Love - 4 - 4

THAT'S AMORE

Words by
JACK BROOKS

Music by
HARRY WARREN

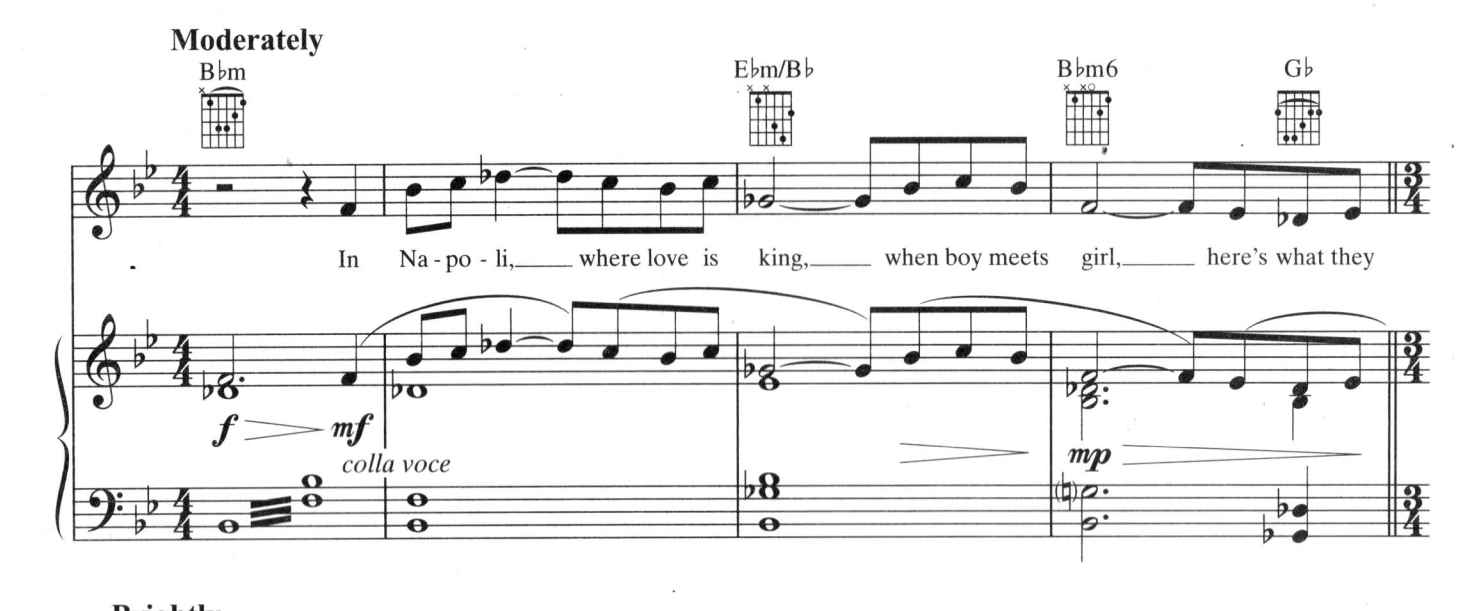

Moderately

In Na-po-li, where love is king, when boy meets girl, here's what they

Brightly

sing: When the

Refrain:

moon hits your eyes like a big piz-za pie, that's a-mo-re.

That's Amore - 4 - 2

tay, tip-py-tip-py-tay, like a gay tar-an-tel-la.___ (Luck-y fel-la.) When the stars make you drool just like pas-ta fa-zool, that's a-mo-re.___ When you dance down the street with a cloud at your feet, you're in love.___

Cm
Ebm6
When you walk in a dream, but you know you're not dream - ing, Si -
cresc. poco a poco
Bb
Dbdim7
F7 Dbdim7
F7 Dbdim7
gno - ré, 'scuz - za me, but you see, back in
f
p mf
mp mf
mp mf
F7
1.
Bb
Cm7/Bb
Bbmaj7
old Na - po - li, that's a - mo - re.
mp
f
mp
Cm7/Bb
2.
Bb
Ebm6
Bb
When the mo - re.
sfz mf
f
mf sfz sfz

THEY CAN'T TAKE THAT AWAY FROM ME

Music and Lyrics by
GEORGE GERSHWIN
and IRA GERSHWIN

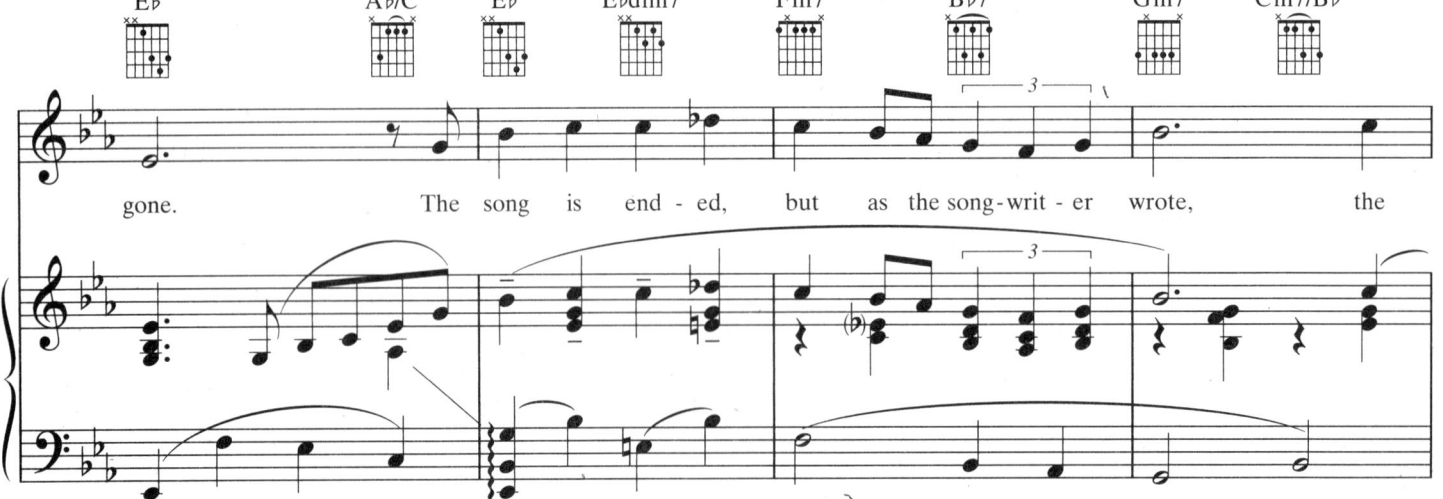

Verse:

Our romance won't end on a sorrowful note, though by tomorrow you're gone. The song is ended, but as the songwriter wrote, the

They Can't Take That Away From Me - 4 - 1

© 1936 (Renewed) GEORGE GERSHWIN MUSIC and IRA GERSHWIN MUSIC
All Rights Administered by WB MUSIC CORP.
All Rights Reserved

Am7 D7 G6 Am7 D13 G6
mel - o - dy lin - gers on. They may take you from me, I'll
Am7 D13 Gm A♭ C7(♯5) Edim7 Fm B♭/D D♭dim7
miss your fond ca - ress. But though they take you from me, I'll still pos -
Refrain: (not fast)
F7 F7(♭5) B♭7 A♭/B♭ E♭6 E♭maj7 E♭/G G♭dim7
sess: The way you wear your hat, the way you sip your tea,
poco marcato
slowly, with warmth
mp – mf
Fm7 B♭7 Fm7 A♭/B♭ E♭7 E9 E♭9 B♭7(♯5) E♭13
the mem-'ry of all that, no, no! They
mf

A♭ Fm7 C9 F7 A♭ A♭/B♭ E♭6 E♭maj7 E♭/G G♭dim7
can't take that a - way from me! The way your smile just beams, the way you sing off key,
mp
Fm7 B♭7 Fm7 A♭/B♭ E♭7 E9 E♭9 B♭7(♯5) E♭13
the way you haunt my dreams, no, no! They
mf
A♭ Fm7 B♭7sus B♭7 E♭6 Gm C9 D7(♭9) Gm C9 D7(♭9)
warmly
can't take that a - way from me! We may nev - er, nev - er meet a - gain on the
con calore
Gm Em7(♭5) A7(♯5) Am7 D7 Gm C9 D7(♭9) Gm B♭m C7
bump-y road to love. Still I'll al - ways, al - ways keep the mem - 'ry

F7 B♭7 A♭ E♭6 E♭maj7 E♭/G G♭dim7
of the way you hold your knife, the way we danced till three,
Fm7 B♭7 Fm7 A♭/B♭ E♭7 E9 E♭9 E♭7sus E♭6 E♭7
the way you've changed my life, no, no! They
A♭ Fm7 B♭7sus B♭7 E♭6 Fm7(♭5) E♭/B♭ Fm7/B♭ B♭13
can't take that a - way from me! No! They can't take that a - way from
1. 2.
E♭ A♭/B♭ E♭ A♭7 B♭7(♭9) E♭6
me! The way you wear your hat, me!
mf f mp mp mf p pp

…

parting,___ this is all I want you to know:___ There

Refrain:

will be man-y oth-er nights like this,___ and I'll be stand-ing

here with some-one new.___ There will be oth-er songs to sing, an-

oth-er fall, an-oth-er spring, but there will nev-er be an-oth-er you.___

There will be other lips that I may kiss, but they won't thrill me like yours used to do. Yes, I may dream a million dreams, but how can they come true, if there will never ever be another you? There you?

There Will Never Be Another You

WALKIN' MY BABY BACK HOME

Words and Music by
FRED AHLERT and ROY TURK

Gee! It's great, af-ter be-in' out late, walk-in' my ba-by back home. Arm in arm, o-ver mead-ow and farm, walk-in' my ba-by back home.

Eb Eb6 Ebmaj7 Eb6 Ebmaj7 Eb6 F9
We go 'long harmonizin' a song, or I'm reciting a poem.
Bb9 Fm7 Bb7 Fm7 Bb7
Owls go by, and they give me the eye, walkin' my baby back
Eb Gm Gm7 C7
home. We stop for awhile, she gives me a smile and
She's 'fraid of the dark, so I have to park out
Eb/Bb Am7(b5) D7sus D7 Gm Gm7
snuggles her head to my chest. We start in to pet, and
side of her door till it's light. She says if I try to

C7 F9 B♭9
that's when I get her tal - cum all o - ver my vest.
kiss her, she'll cry. I dry her tears all through the night.
E♭ E♭6 E♭maj7 E♭6 E♭maj7 E♭6
Af - ter I kind - a straight - en my tie, she has to bor - row my
Hand in hand to a bar - be - cue stand, right from her door - way we
F9 B♭9 Fm7 B♭7
comb. One kiss, then I con - tin - ue a - gain,
roam. Eats! And then it's a plea - sure a - gain,
Fm7 B♭7 1. E♭ G♭dim7 Fm7 B♭ 2. E♭
walk - in' my ba - by back home. home.
walk - in' my ba - by back

WHEN I FALL IN LOVE

Words by
EDWARD HEYMAN

Music by
VICTOR YOUNG

Slowly, with much feeling ♩ = 84

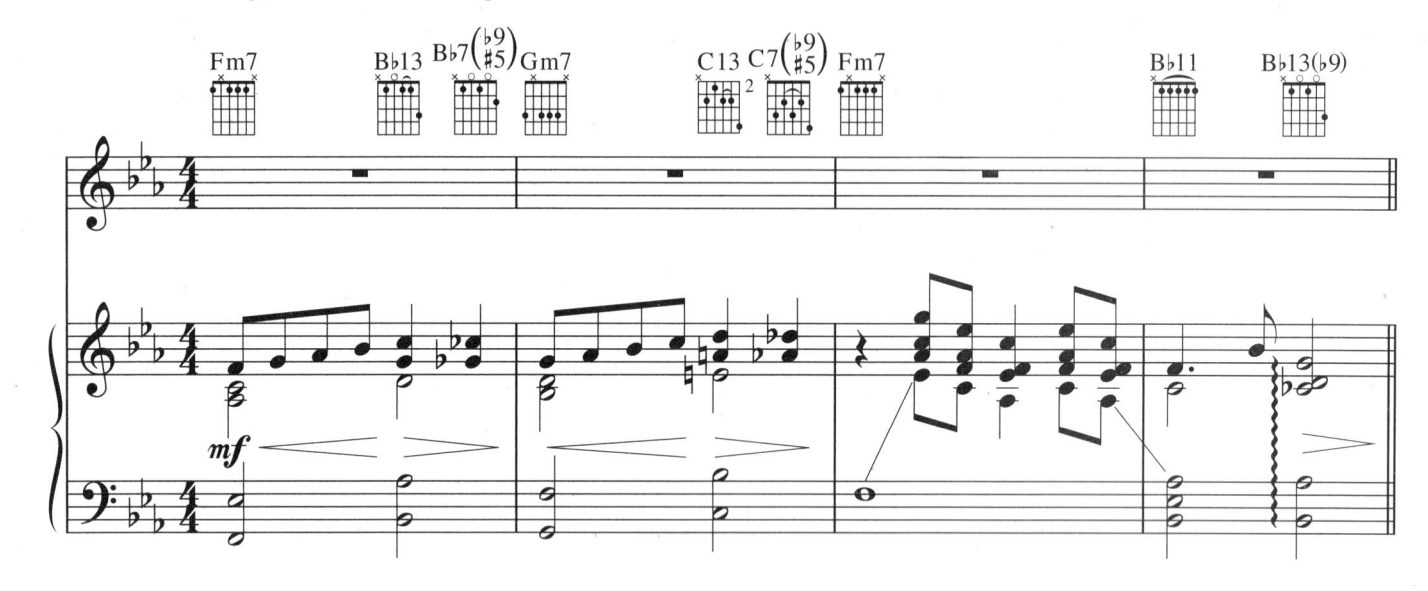

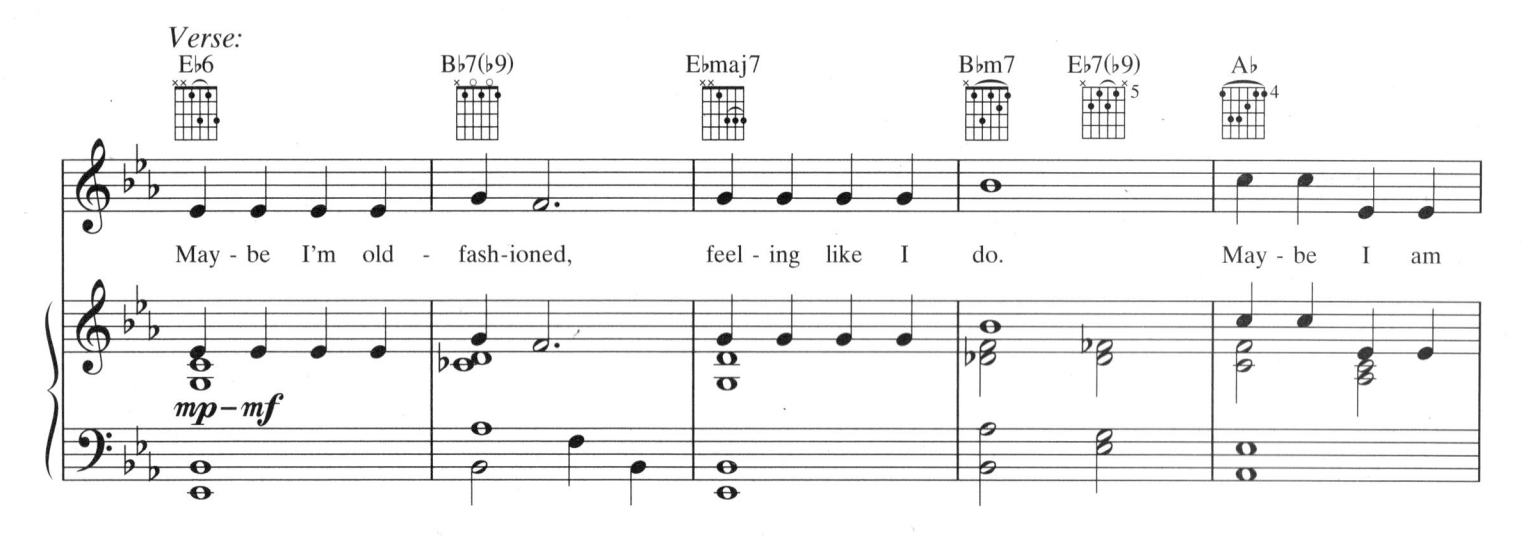

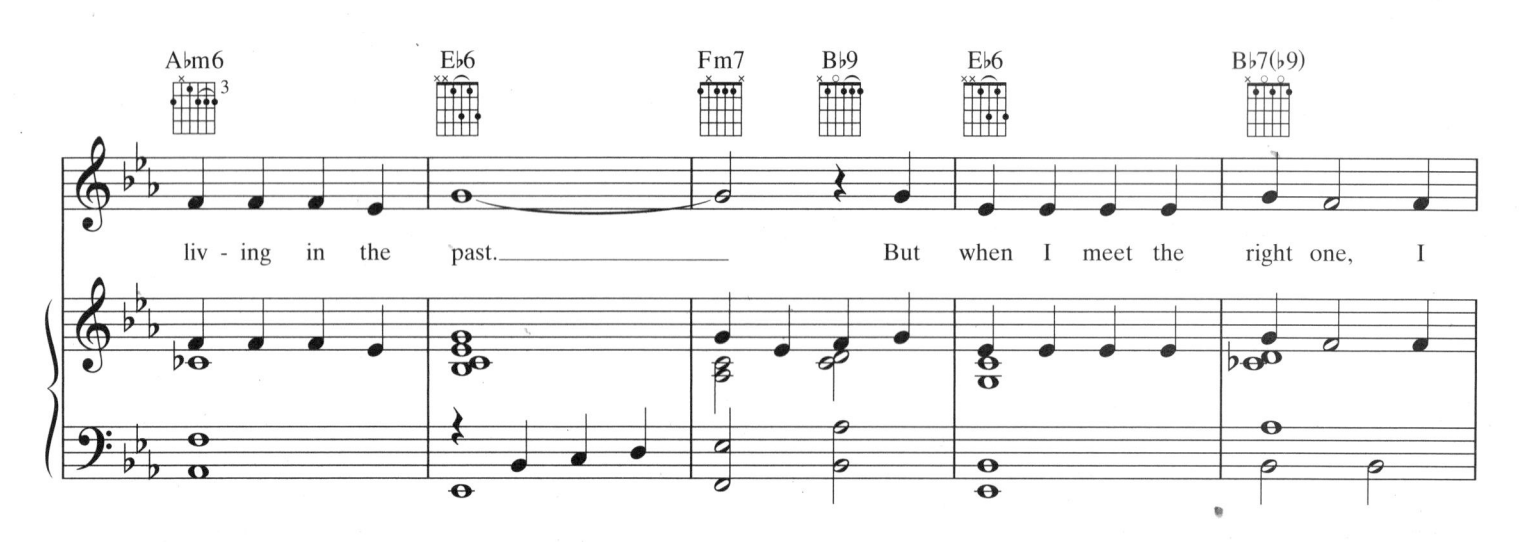

Verse:

May-be I'm old-fash-ioned, feel-ing like I do. May-be I am liv-ing in the past. But when I meet the right one, I

When I Fall in Love - 3 - 1

© 1952 (Renewed) CHAPPELL & CO., INC. and INTERSONG-USA, INC.
All Rights Reserved

know that I'll be true. My first love will be my last.

Chorus:

When I fall in love, it will be for-ev-er, or I'll nev-er fall in love. In a rest-less world like this is, love is end-ed be-fore it's be-gun, and too man-y moon-light kiss-es seem to

Fm Fm7 B♭11 B♭13(♭9) E♭
cool in the warmth of the sun. When I give my heart,
C7(♯5) Fm7 B♭7(♭9) E♭ C7(♯5) Fm7 B♭9 B♭13(♭9)
it will be com - plete - ly, or I'll nev - er give my heart. And the
E♭/G A♭ C7(♯5) C7 C7(♯5) Fm A♭m6 E♭ C7(♭9)
mo - ment I can feel that you feel that way, too, is when I fall in
Fm7 B♭9 B♭7(♭9) E♭6 C13 Fm7 B♭7(♭9) E♭6 Fm7 B♭7(♭9) E♭maj9
1. 2.
love with you. you.
rit.

WORRISOME HEART

Words and Music by
MELODY GARDOT

250

Verses 1 & 2:

1. I___ need a hand   with my wor-ri-some__ heart.___
(2.) break   from my trou-bl-in'___ ways.___

I___ need a hand___
I___ need a break___

___ with my wor-ri-some__ heart.___   I would be luck-
___ from my trou-bl-in'___ ways.___   I would be luck-

Worrisome Heart - 5 - 2

D7
N.C.
y___ to find__ me a man___
y___ to find__ me a man___
who could love me the way that I am
who could love me the way that I am
Gm7 Am7 B♭7 Am7
with this here wor-ri - some__ heart.______
with all my trou-bl - in'___ ways.______
Gm7 Am7
1. B♭7 Am7
2. B♭7 Am7
2. I____ need a
Gm7 Am7 B♭7 Am7 Gm7 Am7
(Inst. ad lib.)

1.
2.
Bb7 Am7 Bb7 Am7
3. I need a
Verse 3:
Gm7 Am7 Bb7 Am7 Gm7 Am7
man who got no bag-gage to claim.
Bb7 Am7 Gm7 Am7 Bb7 Am7
I need a man who got no bag-gage to claim.
Gm7 Am7 Bb7 Am7 D7
I would be luck - y to find me a man

N.C.
who could love me the way that I am, a
Gm7 Am7 Bb7 Am7 Gm7 Am7
wor-ri - some, trou-bl - in', bag-gage-free mod-ern - day dame,
Bb7 Am7 Gm7 Am7 Bb7 Am7
a wor-ri - some, trou-bl - in', bag-gage-free, mod-ern - day dame.
Gm7 Am7 Bb7 Am7 Gm11
Ain't no - bod - y the same.

YOU DON'T KNOW ME

Words and Music by
CINDY WALKER
and EDDY ARNOLD

Moderately slow

You give your hand to me _____ and _____ then you say hel-lo. _____ I can hard-ly speak, _____ my _____ heart is beat-ing so. _____ And an-y-one could tell _____ you think you know me well, _____ but _____ you don't know me. _____ No, _____ you don't know the one _____ who dreams of you at night _____ and longs to

© 1955 (Renewed) MIJAC MUSIC (BMI)
All Rights Administered by WARNER-TAMERLANE PUBLISHING CORP.
All Rights Reserved

kiss your lips____ and longs to hold you tight.___ To you I'm just a friend,____ that's all I've ev-er been,____ but__ you don't know me._____ For I__ nev-er knew the art of mak-ing love,__ though my heart___ aches with love for you. A-fraid__ and shy,_____ I let my chance go by,_____ the chance that you might love me too. You give your hand to me and then you say good-bye. I watch you walk away beside a lucky guy. You'll never, never know the one who loves you so; no, you don't know me. For know me. You'll never, never know the one who loves you so; no, you don't know me.